No B.S.!

John S.

Privacy Means Profit

Privacy Means Profit

Prevent Identity Theft
and Secure You and
Your Bottom Line

John Sileo

WILEY

John Wiley & Sons, Inc.

For general information on our other products and services or for technical support, please contact our Customer Care Department within the United States at (800) 762-2974, outside the United States at (317) 572-3993 or fax (317) 572-4002.

Wiley also publishes its books in a variety of electronic formats. Some content that appears in print may not be available in electronic books. For more information about Wiley products, visit our web site at www.wiley.com.

ISBN 978-0-470-58389-0 (cloth)
ISBN 978-0-470-77052-x (ebk)
ISBN 978-0-470-87224-1 (ebk)
ISBN 978-0-470-87225-x (ebk)

Printed in the United States of America

10 9 8 7 6 5

To my wife Mary,
the strongest, most courageous,
most important person in my life.
I've loved you since I was eight,
and will love you till the day I die.

Contents

For an electronic version of *The Privacy Calendar* (with live links), visit www.Sileo.com/privacy-calendar.

Acknowledgments

During the week that this book is published, it will have been 14 years since I joined my family's 40-year-old business. It will have been exactly 7 years since I found out I could be sent to prison for another man's crimes, and 5 years since those crimes destroyed the family business. This book is the symbol of a delicious victory for so many people; it is tangible proof that we took the bushel of sour lemons handed us and cooked up a sweet lemon pie.

You need to know the truth: One person doesn't write a book. Not even close. I am listed as the author, and get way too much of the credit; but in reality, this accomplishment is as much about others as it is about me. And therein lies the most enjoyable part of writing it: it brought us together like well-written words. I owe everything to those people who stood with me through the ugly times, serving as constant reminders that it *is* okay to trust others.

To Mom and Dad, whom I get to work and play with every day at the business we created out of the ashes. Thanks for being my perfect triumvirate—loving parents, complementary business partners and best friends. (Mom, I left out that comma in honor of you.)

To My Love, who is the coauthor of everything I do. To Sophie and Makayla, you two give me all of the meaning I will ever need in life.

To Liz Crider, who brought this book to completion and kept our business in order as I traveled the world for three months. You are a godsend to our business, and a member of our family.

To Larry Winget, first as my friend, second as my advisor, and third, for getting me this book deal.

To my sister, Andrea, whose wisdom centers me and presence fills me with joy.

To everyone on my team: You each deserve your own line of acknowledgment:

Michael Zinanti, Brad Montgomery, Eric and Karen Peacock, Chris Rogers, John and Kathy Robinson, Peter and Elisabeth Jacobson, Pat Connolly, Mark Throndson, Scott Halford, Steve Spangler, Carly Reed, Lou Heckler, Scott Friedman, Bill Morrow, Nancy Noonan, Diane Sieg, Howard Wallin, Pat Lencioni, Lars Hanson, Michael Santarcangelo, Sue Gwillim, Brian Bostwick, my amazing sister-in-law Julie Walters (who actually read my first book), Fran, Steve, Phil and Sparky Bellio, Jenny Fowler, Lesley Signal, Rachel and Erin Batchelor, Suzanne Vaughan, Geoff Watson, Andrew Kilsby, Linda and Jay Foley, Joseph Fanganello, Dave J., Frank E., Mary B., and everyone at the Department of Defense, and all those mates I've missed. Thank you for your patience, counsel, and friendship.

A special thanks to:

My editor, Daniel Ambrosio (and his team), at John Wiley & Sons, Inc., for putting your faith in me and your hard work into this book.

Jim Van Dyke and everyone at Javelin Strategy & Research for your wonderful reports, sound methodology, and ongoing help.

Larry Ponemon and Mike Spinney of the Ponemon Institute. More than any people I know, you understand the importance of privacy.

All of the bureaus that keep my speaking schedule packed to the gills: Gail Davis & Associates, Washington Speakers Bureau, Goodman Speakers Bureau, FiveStar Speakers, Eagles Talent, Convention Connection, and many others. Thank you for making privacy a profitable profession.

To you, the reader, for being part of the solution.

Boot Camp: Privacy Means Profit

People will do something—including changing their behavior—only if it can be demonstrated that doing so is in their own best interests as defined by their own values.

—Marshall Goldsmith,
What Got You Here Won't Get You There

Motivate the Troops

People don't change bad habits until they have a compelling reason. Too often that compelling reason is the result of a habit's negative outcome; but the promise of positive rewards resulting from the establishment of good habits can be a strong motivator. In the workplace, aligning responsible information stewardship with personal *and* professional gain can set the stage for good privacy habits.

Let My Failure Motivate Your Change

At breakfast on the morning of August 12, 2003, a small and profitable computer company thrived at the foot of the Rocky Mountains. By lunchtime that day, that same business was on its way to ruin. Within 12 months, due to the theft of personal and company information, a 40-year-old family-business-turned-software-startup was doomed, and John, heir to the prosperous enterprise, faced the prospect of prison for crimes he didn't commit.

Beyond the specter of prison time for John, the situation held dire consequences for his family and friends. There was a real threat that his wife and two young daughters might be separated from their husband and father, if John went to prison. John's parents, who founded the company in 1964, shouldered most of the financial responsibility for the dying business and experienced declining health from the resulting stress. In the end, the situation would expose a dark secret kept by John's close friend, Doug, a recent partner in the business.

It sounds like fiction, and sometimes when I'm recounting the ordeal in front of an audience, it *feels* like fiction. But it's 100 percent true. This is the story of how a failure to understand the importance of data privacy not only destroyed a healthy business, but nearly took down an entire family, as well.

If you haven't already figured it out, I am John Sileo, the business leader whose naïve choices brought about the sad saga. Before I experienced it first-hand, I didn't understand that both *individual and business data privacy* are integral to running a profitable company.

What happened to my business, and to me, is more common than you may realize. The statistics throughout this book prove it. The stories I hear from my audiences prove it. But the media headlines continue to ignore it. They minimize massive breaches such as those that occurred at TJX, Heartland Payment Systems, and the U.S. Department of Veterans Affairs with sterile, unemotional language, and they talk about the *risk* of identity theft, but rarely do these stories assess the true toll of identity theft and put a human face on this crime.

Why is the human element missing from these stories? One reason is that victims are often ashamed to openly share their mistakes and failures with the world. Identity theft and its consequences can be humiliating, causing victims to remain quiet. Another reason is that corporations don't want the true emotional costs of information crimes exposed, for fear doing so will awaken a sleeping giant—the complacent public—and you and I might not stand for it any longer. So they call the crime a "data breach," to make it sound technical, hence impersonal. We stay silent, and the business world makes it about numbers instead of lives. But identity theft, or whatever you choose to call it, is highly personal, incredibly invasive, and deeply violating.

There is a great irony underlying the division of this problem between individuals like you and me, and businesses that experience data breach, such as Heartland. We are one and the same. The CEO, responsible for the corporation's data at the highest level, has a Social Security number that is vulnerable to theft. The executive in charge of computer systems that might be hacked, and laptops that might be lost, has a family whose personal medical records could be on those systems. Every human resources administrator responsible for employee records is also an employee whose private financial information is stored in similar files. Every janitor who disposes of sensitive identity documents in the dumpster has identity documents of his own that could be improperly discarded in the trash.

Therein lies the first step in our solution: You must recognize that you could be the victim of this crime just as easily as you could be the source. You are the CEO, the IT manager, the HR administrator, the janitor, the employee, *and* the individual.

Corporate data privacy starts by training a roomful of potential identity theft victims. Teach the CEO and the janitor to understand the destructive emotional and financial impact in personal, human terms that relate directly to them (e.g., the loss of their *own* medical records) and you have the foundation for an effective privacy leader at any level of the organization.

I was forced to make this connection between personal responsibility and workplace responsibility by being the victim *and* the source. I share my story here both as John Sileo, husband and father, and as John Sileo, business executive, so that my pain can guide your progress. Your responsibility is to let my failures motivate and inform your change. I am the example you can hold up to your employees and yourself so that all of you come to understand the consequences of the apathy, ignorance, and inaction that make this a difficult crime to avoid.

This is why you need to read this book, whether you are an individual concerned about guarding your financial well-being or a business leader who is responsible for maintaining the trust and reputation that your employees and customers have placed in you. *You could just as easily be the source as the victim, and it is your responsibility to protect against both.*

The Three Enemies of Privacy: Apathy, Ignorance, and Inaction

When it comes to identity theft and data breach, I'm guessing that your first response is to do nothing. After all, you think, *it's not your fault; it's not your responsibility; it's too difficult a problem.* You have been trained in the behavior of **apathy**: to care little about protecting your private information. In fact, you have been conditioned to give it away without a second thought, armed with excuses as to why you don't need to act: "It won't happen to me." "I'll get to it later." "It's out of my control."

Rubbish.

It is human nature to invest time to prevent tragedy only *after* we've experienced the pain that results from apathy. We hop on the treadmill and order from the healthy menu only *after* our heart screams for attention. We install a home security system only *after* we've been robbed. Pain motivates action, but the damage is usually done.

> *If you know what matters to you, it's easier to commit to change. If you can't identify what matters to you, you won't know when it's being threatened. And in my experience, people only change their ways when what they truly value is threatened.*
>
> —*Marshall Goldsmith,*
> *What Got You Here Won't Get You There (pp. 29–32)*

Similarly, we come to grasp the true value of our personal information only *after* an identity theft or data breach incident occurs that affects us. When your bank calls to tell you that your ATM number was skimmed and your account emptied by a criminal in another state, or when the IRS informs you that your recent tax filing was incorrect because an undocumented worker obtained employment using your Social Security number, the problem becomes personal and you've got a mess on your hands. The good news is that your willingness to read *Privacy Means Profit* sets you apart from the apathetic crowd. By buying this book and learning more about the problem of identity theft, you have taken the first step toward protecting yourself, personally and professionally.

I wasn't so lucky: I ignored my first minor identity theft "heart attack." Just months before my business was destroyed by data theft, I disregarded a warning that should have awakened me to this crime. Days after moving into a new neighborhood, a woman stole my identity out of a garbage bag full of unshredded home-loan documents. "They're just harmless copies," I thought to myself as I threw them out. I didn't even consider identity theft, and I certainly didn't own a shredder.

Using my Social Security number to gain access to my credit profile, the thief purchased her first home (my second) in another state. Unable to keep up with the mortgage payments, she defaulted on the loan and started bankruptcy proceedings—in *my* name. The police declined to investigate (too much of a backlog, they claimed) and I was left alone to endure hundreds of hours cleaning up the mess, filing police reports, repairing my credit, dealing with collection agencies—all on my dime. I ended up spending many weeks of hard-earned vacation time recovering from a crime that could have been prevented with only minutes of effort. My **ignorance** about the real costs of this crime, and even the most basic means of prevention, meant that I had to learn firsthand, the hard and expensive way.

You can learn from my failures, and from the knowledge I gained in the process. In my experience, the most successful people (as measured by happiness, income, and peace of mind), and the most successful businesses (as measured by profitability, customer loyalty, and employee satisfaction) understand that it is easier and *far less expensive* to prevent a disaster than to recover from one. It's why we exercise, teach our kids to respect fire and avoid strangers, diversify our financial investments, and stay out of dark alleys in rough neighborhoods. It's why businesses back up data, perform criminal background checks on job candidates, and provide employee training about many types of risk prevention.

It's no surprise then that successful corporations and insightful individuals apply this same prevention-minded strategy to secure one of their most valuable assets: information. They realize that, in a world where information is currency and knowledge is power, *privacy means profit*.

Privacy means profit applies to both individuals and businesses. The more effectively you protect your private information, the more secure your finances—your personal net worth or your organization's bottom line—will be. I lost nearly $300,000 to identity theft and data breach, and that doesn't even account for the two years I spent recovering rather than earning a salary. Consider the following statistics that illustrate why *privacy means profit*:

- The TJX data breach loss was estimated at *$4.5–$8.6 billion*,[1] at $100 to $182 per breached record, as estimated by experts.
- Heartland Payment Systems stock value declined *64 percent* in the days after it acknowledged a data breach.[2]
- The average data breach costs *$6.75 million* (see Figure 1.1).[3]
- The number of breaches are up *47 percent in a one-year period*.[4]
- In 2008, *285 million records* were breached.[5]
- Of individuals affected by a data breach, *31 percent* will terminate their relationship with the company that lost their information.[6]

The math behind the profitability of privacy is as simple as a profit-and-loss calculation:

$$\text{Revenues} - \text{Expenses} = \text{Profit}$$

Data Theft = Significant Expense (stock depreciation, customer attrition,
lawsuits, victim credit repair, brand damage)
Theft Recovery Expenses > Prevention Expenses

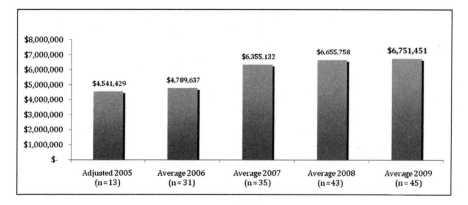

FIGURE 1.1   Average Total Cost of Data Breach by Year

Source: "Fifth Annual U.S. Cost of Data Breach Study," 2010, Ponemon Institute.

In other words, *safe data is profitable data*. And protecting customer data,
employee records, and intellectual property isn't just good business, it's the
right thing to do.

Despite experiencing the actual costs of identity theft at a personal level at
the hands of a dumpster diver, initially I did nothing to further protect myself, nor did I adapt and apply my knowledge at a business level. I gave in to
the final enemy of privacy: **inaction**. It was my refusal to adapt what I had
learned personally to a broader sphere of privacy as it applies to business that
brings us back to the sunny morning of August 12, 2003.

Inaction Destroyed My Business

It was my business decision to form a joint venture with Doug, a business
colleague who had become a close friend while consulting to my computer
company. Together, we built an Internet software business that was profitable
by its third month, providing the lion's share of revenue sustaining our opera-
tions and 11 employees. I was entranced by how profitable we were, by the
financial upside of being a successful entrepreneur in a hot industry, and by
how easily it all came together.

It seemed too good to be true. And so it was.

In the headiness of our success, I failed to verify the credentials of my new friend and business partner. I didn't thoroughly interview his references, question his willingness to jump ship from a stable and lucrative job to a highly risky venture, or perform even a simple criminal background check. It didn't seem necessary; after all, Doug worked harder and for longer hours than anyone else in the company. Eventually, I gave him access to the company computer systems, accounting software, and bank accounts. He knew many of my passwords, had access to personal files in my office, and enjoyed the privileges of trust with little monitoring of his activities. He was such a good fit as a business partner that my wife and father both commented prophetically that he was *too good to be true*. At one point, my father even advised that he wouldn't put his trust in a business partner until that trust was earned, and that earning trust should take at least five years.

I agreed, but thinking something and acting on it are two entirely different things.

I realize that handing over so much control so quickly must seem terribly naïve to you—and it was (in this case, naïveté that was the by-product of *apathy*, *ignorance*, and *inaction*). Yet I see the same story replay itself over and over again in businesses much larger than mine. After all, Doug was a friend and a very intelligent man, and he knew how to use those qualities to *engineer my trust*. We worked together almost two years before he started taking advantage of me, all the while treating me like family.

Doug used my unprotected identity and the company's private customer data to embezzle nearly $300,000 from our clients over the course of 18 months. On August 12, 2003, during a phone call, our biggest client threatened to put me in jail for the thefts, since it was my name that appeared throughout the criminal paper trail. Several days later, an investigator from the Denver District Attorney's office contacted me and started what would become a two-year battle to prove my innocence and stay out of jail.

During that time, our software business failed (despite being profitable even without embezzled income), the 40-year-old family computer business failed, and I lived under the constant cloud of possibly going to prison for crimes I didn't commit.

I was, however, guilty of one thing: refusing to take responsibility for the safety of personal and business data.

Despite the huge financial losses we suffered, the most painful aspects of this ordeal turned out to be the two years of quality time I lost with my wife and kids while fighting business battles, the negative effects it had on my parent's health, and the deep bitterness I felt at being betrayed by a close friend. *Money can always be earned back; time and relationships cannot.*

After a stint in a psychiatric hospital, Doug eventually went to jail, but for only 18 days. His sentence didn't feel like justice to me; nevertheless, and even after all he put me and my family through, I made the decision to focus on *what I could control* rather than the severity of Doug's punishment. After two cases of identity theft and two years of recovery, I finally took responsibility for protecting my identity and the identities touched by my business.

Eventually, from the ashes of my former profession rose a new career, a new life, and a new respect for privacy. Passing what I have learned on to audiences around the world—and to you—is the only fitting justice for this ordeal.

Business Relevance

As a business leader, it is essential that you clearly understand the relationship between identity theft, data breach, and your bottom line. Here is a crash course, from my perspective.

One of the costliest data security mistakes I see executives make is to initially approach data privacy from the perspective of the company. They don't recognize the following reality: *All privacy is personal*.

In other words, no one in your organization will care about data security, privacy policies, intellectual property protection, or data breach until they understand *what it has to do with them*. If your employees and executives don't care about protecting their own identities (to prevent identity theft), how can you expect them to care about protecting corporate identity (to prevent data breach)? Like the emergency oxygen masks on a depressurized airplane, it's important to put your own on first, or you'll be worthless to those around you. *Protecting yourself first isn't self-centered; it's effective and educational*. Security begins at the human level and expands outward to the group level.

I recently delivered a speech at the Pentagon as part of an ongoing financial literacy campaign run by the Department of Defense. After the speech, an Air Force commander asked me why he was having such a hard time convincing his younger soldiers to protect sensitive military data. Their risky behavior included inadvertently tweeting troop locations, posting photos of fellow soldiers on their Facebook walls, and surfing on unprotected wireless networks. The problem, which has been publicly documented, has led the Pentagon to ban social networking from at least one branch of the military (at time of publication).

When I asked the commander how many of his men and women had been trained to understand the value of protecting their own personal information (i.e., how many had just attended the financial literacy event), he immediately drew the connection: *Good personal privacy habits lead to good professional privacy practices*. Change always takes place at the personal level first.

The end game for business leaders is to build a Culture of Privacy within their organizations, to make security part of the daily fabric, part of the mission and vision of their companies. A Culture of Privacy exists when every member of the organization (especially the CEO) *believes* in the need to protect his or her own private information, *as well as* customer data, employee records, and intellectual property.

This foundation of belief is clearly lacking among corporate executives. Look at the key findings of the Ponemon Institute/Ounce Labs study, "Business Case for Data Protection," which surveyed C-level executives (CEO, CFO, COO, CIO, CSO, etc.) about data protection inside of their corporations (emphasis mine):

- Of the C-level executives surveyed *82 percent* said that their organizations had experienced a *data breach*, and many of them are *positive they cannot prevent a repeat performance*.
- Of the CEOs surveyed, *53 percent* said that the CIO is responsible for data protection, yet only *24 percent* of the other C-levels would point to the CIO as the one responsible for data protection overall.
- Of those who are said to be in charge of data protection, *85 percent* don't believe that a *failure to stop a data breach would impact their job*.

(continued)

(*continued*)

In other words, C-level executives admit that a breach has already happened, are fairly certain it will happen again, recognize they are unprepared to stop a recurrence, and yet can't clearly identify who will be held responsible; nor do they feel that they will be held accountable when the inevitable happens. At this stage, building a Culture of Privacy is mostly bluster.

The result is that many organizations try to implement privacy policies and practices without actually believing in their mission. Instead of fostering a voluntary Culture of Privacy, they end up force-feeding an involuntary Regime of Privacy, and fall back into apathy when the fear wears off.

The most effective way to build a Culture of Privacy is to break it down into three simple steps (most corporations skip the first step, dooming them to failure):

1. *Motivate the individual.* Train your employees and executives on how to protect their own information *first*. Learning the basic principles of privacy at an individual level is a prerequisite for all subsequent forms of data security, and supplies the necessary motivation to apply the same habits at work. All employees need to overcome their own apathy, ignorance, and inaction before they are equipped to protect corporate assets. *This book is aimed at making it personal. By learning to protect their own identities, your executives and employees are acquiring the building blocks necessary to construct a corporate Culture of Privacy.* Identity theft training is good for their wellness, and is a means to a safer and more profitable end.

2. *Empower the team.* Employees alone do not have the authority or resources to act. By empowering cross-departmental teams (who already understand privacy at a personal level) with the authority and resources to focus on low-hanging security fruit (e.g., laptop computers, document shredding, wireless surfing), you make immediate progress and win crucial organizational buy-in. In contrast, organizations with a Regime of Privacy tend to force data security into a silo (e.g., "It's the IT department's responsibility"—see

statistics cited previously), never taking into account the vital role played by legal counsel, compliance officers, the CFO, human resources, and even facilities maintenance. In a Culture of Privacy, the team is integrated, and the results are more enduring.

3. *Lead by example.* There is nothing that undermines a Culture of Privacy faster than an executive team that doesn't practice what they preach. A CEO who surfs unprotected in the airport, or refuses to invest in deskside shredders, will send a hypocritical message echoing throughout the corporation: "Privacy doesn't really matter; we're just going through the motions." In the same manner, a CEO who appoints some form of chief data protection officer but doesn't supply the vision, budget, or authority to make it happen is the same CEO whose data breach catastrophe shows up on the front page of the *Wall Street Journal.*

Look closely at the Contents for *Privacy Means Profit.* The chapter headings provide a road map for the individual steps to take in building your Culture of Privacy. Begin with a privacy boot camp, where you *motivate* change before you demand it. *Define* what data is at risk, where it lives, and why it needs to be protected. *Engage* your troops with simple, memorable tools. During basic training, teach them to *eliminate, destroy, secure, lock, evaluate, interrogate,* and *monitor* at-risk information. Don't try to implement the strategy overnight. Instead, target the enemy by *adapting, accumulating, and prioritizing* your security campaigns. These are the skills you will develop at a personal level by reading the remainder of this book.

How to Get the Most Out of This Book

You will notice that this book is organized differently from other books on identity theft, which are typically structured around tasks and to-do lists (e.g., protecting your mail, shredding documents, etc.). While *Privacy Means Profit* covers all of those tasks in the Action Items feature of each chapter, it embeds them within broader concepts of protection such as *eliminate, destroy, lock*, and so forth. These mind-sets can then be easily adapted and applied in the workplace.

By training you at the conceptual level and reinforcing what you learn with very specific action items to complete, you will walk away with a much broader and more flexible understanding of protecting yourself and your workplace. Giving you only checklists won't protect you over the long term, because identity thieves change their methods of attack, rendering any static checklist obsolete as soon as it is printed. By learning the concepts, you will have a dynamic skill-set to apply both today and in the future, at home and at work.

Each chapter contains three features:

The Mind-set: The first layer of protection is a mind-set, or a habitual way of thinking about your private information that will trigger alarms in your head when your identity is at risk. For example, instead of having to remember to shred lists of specific documents, you will develop the habit of destroying any private information that will be handled by others. I describe this mind-set as "think like a spy," and I will explain it in detail in Part II.

Action Item Checklist: The second layer of protection is a series of specific action items (to-do steps) that should be completed to protect your personal identity. I use the action items in each chapter to illustrate and reinforce exactly how you start to think like a spy. When you are shredding old bank statements, for example, you aren't just checking an item off your action list. You are reinforcing the habit of destroying anything with a piece of your identity on it that you no longer need. These action items are based on statistical data showing how identities are most commonly stolen and who steals them. The action items provide the most immediate and practical form of protection.

Business Relevance: In relevant chapters, I bridge the knowledge of how to protect yourself personally with how to expand that into your workplace. For example, once you have learned to properly shred sensitive documents at home, it is much easier to apply a more sophisticated form of shredding at work. This feature is targeted primarily at business leaders who are trying to protect their organizations against data breach and workplace identity theft, but it will be informative for individuals as well. *If you are an employee at a corporation, association, university, or* *small business, you must realize that protecting organizational data is vital not only to your company's profitability, but for your job security.*

Give a man a fish and you feed him for a day. Teach a man to fish and you feed him for a lifetime.

—*Lao Tzu*

By reading *Privacy Means Profit* both for the concepts as well as the action items, you will learn to "fish" for yourself. If you are anxious to complete the checklists first (i.e., feed yourself today), skip to Chapter 16, "Prioritize Your Attack: The Privacy Calendar," and return to the other chapters as you have time.

2

Define the Problem

Until we know exactly what we need to be protecting, we are simply wasting time and money. The most cost-effective and efficient way to implement change begins with defining terms and outlining a plan of attack. This chapter looks at what makes up identity in its entirety, where it "lives," and how it is stolen.

What Is Identity?

In the realm of daily life, identity is how we define or describe ourselves—as a mother, wife, piano player, author, and so on. But in the realm of privacy and "identity theft," we focus on a subset of identity called *data identity*, which is how others, usually companies, associations, or governments, define or reference us. For the purposes of this book, however, I will refer to data identity simply as *identity*.

Identity is made up of any name, number, or attribute that provides information on us or allows access into further personal data about us. Identity is almost always used to link us to money, special privileges, or access. For example, our Social Security number connects us to our credit file, retirement and unemployment benefits, and tax obligations. According to the "2009 Identity Fraud Survey Report," Social Security numbers top the list of compromised data among victims, at 38 percent.[1] Frequent-flyer numbers give access to our accrued mileage and membership benefits; supermarket loyalty cards to our buying habits and product preferences. Technology has made it easier to replicate these forms of identity for fraudulent purposes. High-resolution scanners and printers have made reproducing licenses, checks, and other identity documents a simple affair for identity thieves.

> *Identity [f]raud is rising and has reported an increase in crimes of opportunity mostly due to economic misfortune and the need for immediate gains. This increase is supported by an increasingly global, hierarchal, specialized criminal enterprise, as well as the upsurge of a secondary market for financial information and the availability of inexpensive toolkits for defrauding that can make anyone a professional identity thief.*
>
> —*"2009 Identity Fraud Survey Report" (p. 9),*
> *Javelin Strategy & Research*

As older identity technologies are compromised, newer forms will appear, such as biometrics. For example, it is becoming more common that our fingerprints and voice patterns are used to identify and distinguish us. These forms of identity verification mechanisms have drawbacks and can be compromised as well, which is why we need to progress beyond simple checklists into habits of privacy that apply to any technology.

The following is a comprehensive (but not exhaustive) list of the items, numbers, and attributes that define our identities. I have left blank spaces at the end for you to include additional pieces of your identity makeup. It is important that you study this list, as it is the foundation for the rest of the book. If you don't know what comprises your identity, and define what is at risk, you won't be able to protect it from thieves.

- ❏ Social Security number
- ❏ Full name
- ❏ Aliases, nicknames ("nics"), pseudonyms ("nyms"), also-known-as'es (AKAs)
- ❏ Current address(es)
- ❏ Prior addresses
- ❏ Family members' names and contact information
- ❏ Driver's license number
- ❏ Date of birth
- ❏ Bank account number(s)

- ❏ Investment account number(s)
- ❏ Computer password(s)
- ❏ Internet password(s)
- ❏ Credit card number(s)
- ❏ Debit card numbers(s)
- ❏ Insurance policy number(s)
- ❏ ATM PIN(s)
- ❏ Phone number(s)
- ❏ Cell number(s)
- ❏ E-mail address(es)
- ❏ Username(s)
- ❏ Mother's maiden name
- ❏ Historical information (high school mascot, etc.)
- ❏ Biometrics
  - ❏ Photographs
  - ❏ Video
  - ❏ Fingerprint
  - ❏ Footprint
  - ❏ Iris scan
  - ❏ Retinal scan
  - ❏ Gait profile (identifies the particular and unique way you walk)
  - ❏ Facial scan
  - ❏ Voice pattern
  - ❏ Tissue samples
  - ❏ DNA
- ❏ Height, weight, hair and eye color
- ❏ Sex
- ❏ Ethnicity
- ❏ Nationality
- ❏ Citizenship
- ❏ Computer IP address(es)
- ❏ Occupation
- ❏ Loyalty numbers (e.g., frequent flyer, grocery)
- ❏ Garage door and alarm codes
- ❏ Religion
- ❏ Political affiliations
- ❏ Memberships

- ☐ Custody papers
- ☐ Court orders
- ☐ _____
- ☐ _____
- ☐ _____

On Your Computer

- ☐ Contact manager and e-mail programs (e.g., Outlook, Apple's Address Book, ACT)
- ☐ Software (e.g., Quicken, Money)
- ☐ CD-ROMS and DVDs
- ☐ Floppy disks
- ☐ USB thumb drives
- ☐ Across wireless networks
- ☐ Across Bluetooth devices
- ☐ Spreadsheets
- ☐ PDFs
- ☐ Word documents
- ☐ PowerPoint documents

Online

- ☐ Online retailers (e.g., Amazon)
- ☐ Financial institutions (e.g., banks, brokerages, credit unions, insurance companies)
- ☐ Google (e.g., Gmail, Contacts, Search History, Calendar)
- ☐ Social networks (e.g., Facebook, MySpace, LinkedIn, Twitter)
- ☐ Online bill pay services
- ☐ Directory services (e.g., Spokeo.com, Zabasearch.com, Intelius.com, Pipl.com, Whitepages.com)
- ☐ Reunion websites (e.g., Classmates.com)
- ☐ "Find a friend" websites

In Your Car

- ☐ Car registration
- ☐ Proof of insurance

☐ Repair receipts

☐ _____

☐ _____

☐ _____

At Work

☐ Customer data
☐ Personnel records
☐ Intellectual capital
☐ Trade secrets
☐ Computer
☐ Identification cards
☐ Company cell phone

☐ _____

☐ _____

☐ _____

In Public

☐ Government documents (e.g., birth certificates, driver's license number, addresses, real estate records, Social Security number, criminal records, property tax rolls, income tax documents, vehicle registration, passport)
☐ Licensing entities (fishing, hunting, driver's, marriage)
☐ Property deeds and records
☐ Criminal records

In Data Warehouses and Businesses

Businesses keep records on us to sell to other businesses for marketing purposes or to market directly to us, such as:

☐ Credit bureaus (e.g., Experian, Equifax, TransUnion, Innovis)
☐ Data aggregators (e.g., ChoicePoint, Lexis/Nexis, Acxiom)
☐ Retail stores
☐ Credit card companies

In Our Brains!

☐ We store much of our identity information in our heads and share it verbally.

How Individuals' Identities Are Stolen (It's Not All Cybercrime)

From listening to the media, you would think that the Internet and cybercrime are to blame for most cases of identity theft. Statistics, however, prove they are not. *Cybercrime accounts for only 11 percent of actual identity fraud* cases, according to the latest Javelin Strategy & Research study,[1] and online shopping accounts for a meager *1 percent!* When it comes to victims having their identity stolen when making in-store purchases, women have a 94 percent incidence rate, and men only a 43 percent rate. This is attributed primarily to the fact that women shop more in stores, whereas men shop more online (or not at all).

There is an important lesson in this confusion between reality and perception: Don't automatically believe everything you hear, especially in the media (see Chapter 8, "Evaluate the Risk"). It's sexy to write about cybercrime, but the disproportionate amount of attention it receives gives us a false sense that it is the leading cause of identity theft.

The following summarizes the results of the 2009 Javelin Strategy & Research findings on how your identity information was obtained:[2]

- *Technology plays a smaller* role in identity theft than we perceive.
- Most known cases of fraud are committed when the criminal has *direct, physical access to the victim's information.*
- Of identity theft cases where the victims knew how their information was obtained, *43 percent* were the result of a *lost or stolen* wallet, checkbook, credit card, or physical document—which means you can remove almost half of your risk by following the guidelines in Chapter 4, "Eliminate the Source," alone.
- *Thirty-one percent* of identity theft cases happen because another institution mishandles a victim's data (i.e., data breach).
- *Friends and family* members are the thieves in a significant number of identity theft cases.

With those statistics in mind, let's apply the *profitability of privacy* formula to each layer of protection based on estimated percentages of reported cases of identity theft gathered from a number of sources, as shown in the following table. For the sake of this exercise, imagine that your identity is worth $100,000. (On average, it is worth far more than that, but setting the value at this figure makes the math easier.) As you apply each layer of protection (thereby lessening the dollar amount stolen by the corresponding percentage of the crime), your risk diminishes to a point where stealing your identity is no longer attractive to criminals. They are better served moving on to the next victim, who has done nothing to protect his or her identity.

Profitability of Your Identity to a Thief as You Begin to Protect Yourself

Solution	% of Risk Reduction	Value of Your Identity to a Thief
No protections taken	NA	$100,000
Protect your *wallet, checks, credit cards, and* take steps to minimize damage, in case they are stolen. (*Eliminate*)	35	$65,000
Lock up or *destroy* identity lying around your home, for friends and family to steal. (*Lock, Destroy*)	15	$50,000
Protect your *computer* from viruses, spyware, botnets, and hackers. (*Secure*)	20	$30,000
Know how to prevent *retail* identity theft in restaurants, stores, and in any other circumstance your credit card leaves your sight. (*Evaluate*)	15	$15,000
Protect incoming and outgoing *mail.* (*Lock, Destroy*)	5	$10,000
Cut in half the amount of data you make available to businesses that could become the source of data theft. (*Evaluate, Interrogate*)	5	$5,000
Your identity is now worth *1/20 of its original value*, giving the thief greater incentive to move on to another victim, rather than to continue to wring dollars out of your data.		

Defining Common Methods of Theft

What methods do identity thieves use? Where are you vulnerable? The more you know about criminal methods, the louder the alarms will ring when you encounter one of these situations. In the list here I describe a number of the common methods thieves use to steal identities. Following each method, enclosed in parentheses and set in boldface (e.g., **Monitor**) is the mind-set you need to assume to help you combat the particular method.

ATM Skimming: A spy installs a "skimmer" on an ATM machine to capture your card number, expiration date, name, and other valuable information. Coupled with shoulder surfing (or a hidden camera), this gives a spy everything he or she needs to drain your bank account. **(Evaluate)**

Cell Phone Cloning: A cloned cell phone is reprogrammed to transmit the electronic serial number and telephone number of a legitimate cell phone, which is then billed for the calls made from the cloned cell phones. **(Monitor)**

Computer Hacking: A spy uses spyware, viruses, or hacking tools to access the information on your computer—usually passwords, credit card numbers, and bank accounts. **(Secure)**

Cross-site Scripting: An existing website's vulnerabilities are exploited to download malware onto the computers of users who visit the website. **(Secure)**

Data Breach: An organization (corporation, nonprofit, association, government, university) loses your private information (e.g., Heartland Payment Systems, TJX). Many times it is stolen by one of the other methods. **(Monitor)**

Dumpster Diving: A spy (or thief) rummages through your home or business garbage looking for documents that allow them to exploit existing accounts or set up new credit card accounts, establish phone service, drain bank accounts, take out loans, and more. **(Destroy)**

Evil Twinning: A spy sets up a wireless network identical to the one at your favorite wireless hotspot (e.g., an Internet café). When you log on to the network, the hacker is able to browse your computer and steal data. **(Secure)**

Friendly Fraud: A friend, family member, contract laborer, or domestic help (here, the spy) takes identity documents out of your home or business, or copies down information and leaves the materials. These are the most difficult criminals to catch, and their crimes carry the highest price tag. These types of thieves often use the information they steal to file bankruptcy, take out a car loan, pay drug or gambling debts, or present an alternate identity if they are arrested. **(Eliminate, Destroy, Secure, Lock, Monitor)**

Keylogging: Spyware that captures every keystroke an individual makes on a computer (login information, passwords, account numbers, etc.). Keyloggers are rampant on public computers (such as those in the library, hotel business centers, and Internet cafés). **(Secure)**

Midnight Mailing: A spy cuts a hole in the bottom of blue U.S. Postal Service mailboxes and regularly picks up mail, generally to "wash" checks (using fingernail polish remover to change the Pay To field so that the check can be made out to the thief). Many times, thieves just steal the entire box in the middle of the night and replace it by morning. **(Lock)**

Old-fashioned Stealing: A spy steals or finds your lost wallet, purse, checkbook, credit card, driver's license, passport, and so on. They also pick up credit card receipts and checks left on restaurant tables. **(Eliminate, Evaluate)**

Pharming: Computer hackers temporarily take over website addresses and make you think you are entering information at your bank or other financial institution when you are actually doing so on the hacker's data collection site. They then use this data to break into your real accounts. Knowing how they do this is less important than learning how to protect against it. **(Secure, Monitor)**

Phishing: A spy sends you an e-mail that appears to be from a familiar source, such as your bank, PayPal, eBay, your brokerage, and the like. The spy asks you to fill out a form with your personal information and uses it to break into your real account. **(Evaluate, Interrogate)**

Pretexting: A thief calls a financial institution under false pretenses (pretending to be someone he or she isn't, including you). For example, a pretexter might call a bank and pose as a customer, to obtain sensitive information. **(Secure, Lock)**

Red-Flagging: A spy steals the mail from your home or business mailbox, usually to apply for preapproved credit cards, intercept new credit and debit cards, and to steal your new checks. Putting up the red flag on your home mailbox (hence, the name) signals identity thieves that it is time to steal. Leaving incoming or outgoing mail stacked in your e-mail inbox or work mailbox is an open invitation for workplace identity theft. **(Lock)**

Shoulder Surfing: A spy peers over your shoulder at an ATM machine or grocery store to obtain your PIN number. He or she often records your actions using a cell phone video camera. **(Evaluate)**

Skimming: A spy (in this case, a waiter, retail clerk, etc.) legitimately processes your credit card but then swipes it through a handheld "skimmer" to subsequently use for credit card fraud. (**Evaluate, Monitor**)

SMiShing: Phishing applied to the texting world. This type of theft uses cell phone text messages to deliver the "bait," which entices you to divulge your personal information. The "hook" (the method used to actually "capture" your information) in the text message may be a website URL, as in related phishing schemes. However, it has become more common to receive a texted phone number that connects to an automated voice response system. (**Evaluate**)

Social Engineering: A spy manipulates data out of victims by convincing the unwitting that they are trustworthy and have our best interests at heart. (**Evaluate, Interrogate**)

Synthetic Identity Fraud: Identity thieves build a new identity by combining pieces of identity gathered from multiple sources (including you). For example, they might use your Social Security number and someone else's name and address. These files are then tagged as subfiles on victims' credit reports, who generally won't take notice until they apply for credit, try to take out a loan, or, in some cases, are contacted by debt collectors. (**Monitor, Lock, Secure, Destroy**)

Trojan Horse: A computer program is made to appear as a legitimate file or software upgrade from a reliable source, thereby tricking the victim into opening it. The Trojan horse gives intruders access to the personal information stored on that computer. (**Secure**)

Vishing: A form of phishing that uses both e-mail and telephone, or just telephone. Usually, the victim is urged to resolve an account issue and divulge personal information to a thief posing as a representative of a financial institution. (**Evaluate, Interrogate**)

Wardriving: A spy (or war driver) drives around neighborhoods looking for unprotected wireless networks. When such a network is discovered, he or she uses the Internet connection to commit crimes (usually associated with pornography or methamphetamines) or to browse your computer and steal information. (**Secure**)

Figure 2.1 estimates the total dollar value gained by thieves using some of these methods.

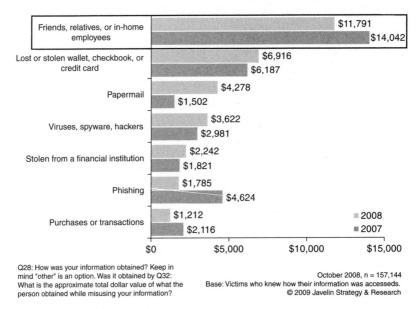

Q28: How was your information obtained? Keep in mind "other" is an option. Was it obtained by Q32: What is the approximate total dollar value of what the person obtained while misusing your information?

October 2008, n = 157,144
Base: Victims who knew how their information was accessed.
© 2009 Javelin Strategy & Research

FIGURE 2.1 Cost of Recovery by Source of Theft

Source: "Identity Fraud on the Rise But Consumer Costs Plummet as Protections Increase," Javelin Strategy & Research, January 2009.

The Five Main Types of Identity Theft

The five main types of identity theft are:

- Financial
- Social Security number
- Character/criminal
- Medical
- Driver's license

Financial

Financial identity theft is the most common and publicized form of identity theft, and takes many forms. Some ID thefts occur when a credit or debit card, bank account or brokerage account number, or checks are stolen.

Thieves taking a more tactical approach will complete a change-of-address form at the post office and have credit cards in your name sent to the new address. Or a criminal may complete a preapproved credit card offer sent to you in the mail, using your name, date of birth, and Social Security number, but have the card sent to a different address they indicate on the application form. Identity thieves also access your credit card and purchase information through fraudulent or unsecured websites.

Check fraud often begins when the thief breaks into your mailbox. Sophisticated thieves will forge your checks, or use the aforementioned check-washing technique to change the amount and payee.

Other financial forms of identity theft include: new account fraud, loan fraud, payday loan schemes, Nigerian scams, and Social Security benefits fraud, among others.

Social Security Number

Your Social Security number can hold the key to your entire identity, both personally and financially. If a thief gets ahold of your Social Security number, he or she can use it in a variety of ways. The most popular are to:

- Gain employment
- Open new lines of credit (loans, credit card accounts, bank accounts)
- Drain your Social Security benefits so that at retirement you have nothing.

Social Security identity theft is particularly difficult to recover from.

Character/Criminal

A criminal can potentially take over your entire character and commit crimes in your name. In these types of crimes, victims may not even know that their identity has been hijacked until they are pulled over or receive a knock on their front door, to learn from the police that multiple warrants are out for their arrest.

Medical

Your medical insurance can be stolen, after which the thief racks up medical bills in your name. This type of identity theft can be hard to detect, especially if you don't make frequent visits to doctors. Not only can this type of identity theft result in a financial mess and be highly time-consuming, it can also be life-threatening. If, for example, a thief's blood type is appended to your record, and you should one day need a transfusion, you could receive the wrong type of blood.

> *Despite much of the hype surrounding "medical identity theft," the data shows that relatively few fraud victims are impacted by the theft of such information. This area may expand as more American's lose their employment and health insurance benefits.*
>
> —*"2009 Identity Fraud Report,"*
> *Javelin Strategy & Research*

In spite of the quote above, it would be unwise to assume that medical identity theft can be ignored. It might not appear to be a significant problem now, but I am confident that it is becoming a more commonplace and destructive form of identity theft every day.

Driver's License

An identity thief can steal your driver's license then rent, purchase, or register a vehicle in your name. If he or she subsequently gets into a car accident, you could be held responsible. Even a simple traffic violation or DUI will be attached to your record, not the thief's. Keep in mind, a stolen purse or wallet is the major cause of identity theft, making driver's license theft rather common.

Business Relevance

Identity theft describes what happens to the individual, you and me, when our private identifying information is stolen. Data breach describes what happens when that *same information* is stolen from a corporation, organization, association, university, or government agency. For the most part, the terms *identity theft* and *data breach* describe the same crime from two different perspectives (one personal, the other corporate).

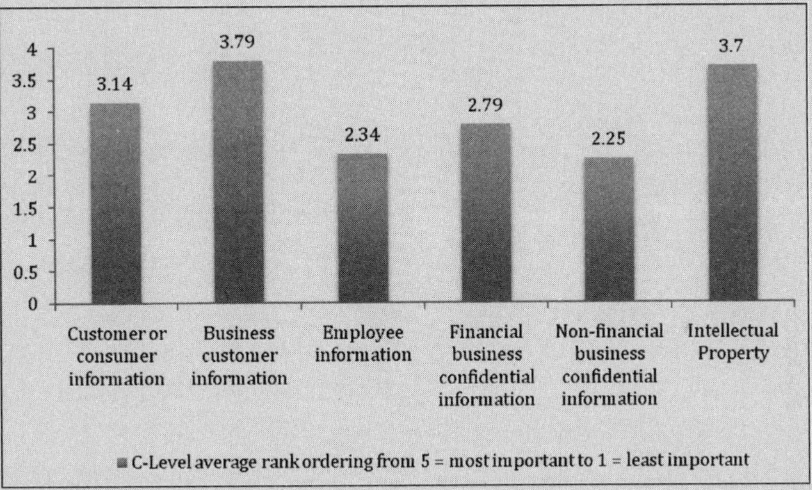

FIGURE 2.2   Average Rank of Data Believed to Be Most Critical to the Organization's Operation

Source: "Fifth Annual U.S. Cost of Data Breach Study," Ponemon Institute, 2010.

All the identity types and sources described in this chapter as being at risk of theft are the same pieces of information that are at risk of data breach. A criminal wants to steal your Social Security number whether it is from you personally (identity theft) or from a corporate database (data breach), in order to commit identity theft.

The point here for businesses is to teach their employees and executives to identify sensitive forms of business identity by first understanding the corresponding risks of exposing their own identity data. In other words, if an employee at your company reads this chapter and learns to define what makes up her own identity, so that she can protect herself personally, she has also just familiarized herself with a majority of the types of data that she needs to protect at your company.

(continued)

(continued)
    That said, there are several additional types of information that can be stolen from businesses that don't have a direct personal equivalent:

- Intellectual property
- Trade secrets
- Profit-and-loss statements
- Balance sheets
- Cash flow analyses
- Business strategies
- Marketing initiatives
- Pending mergers and acquisitions
- Organizational structure

According to the Ponemon Institute, more than half (56 percent) of an organization's sensitive or confidential information is contained on paper documents. Also, 53 percent of employees very often put this sensitive information at risk by leaving these documents at communal printers, in meeting rooms, or at meetings held outside of the office.

—"Security of Paper Documents in the Workplace,"
Ponemon Institute, October 2008, p. 5

Failure to Define

Many organizations fail to *define the problem* as it relates to their company. By answering the questions here, you will begin to familiarize yourself with what you must know about the data inside your business in order to protect it. Defining the problem, even roughly, will begin to give you a framework of risk against which to apply the remainder of the lessons provided in this book.

1. *List exactly what sensitive information exists inside your business.* Be specific. Use the checklists given in this chapter as a starting point, then customize the lists to meet the specific requirements of your organization.

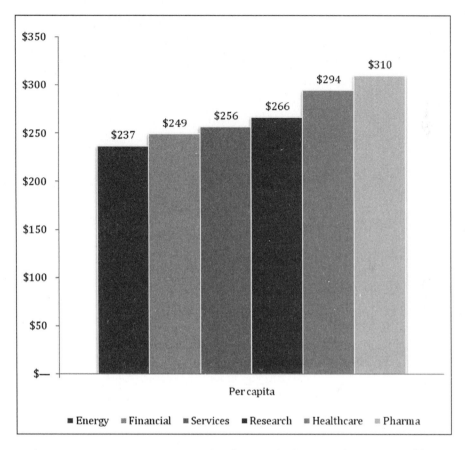

FIGURE 2.3 Cost per Compromised Record of a Breach Compared by Industry Classification

Source: "Fifth Annual U.S. Cost of Data Breach Study," Ponemon Institute, 2010.

2. *Itemize where that data "lives," physically and digitally.* List every possible source as specifically as possible (e.g., CRM database, accounting system, point-of-sale system, HR files, filing cabinets, computers, laptops, servers, digital archives, CDs, DVDs, tape backups, thumb drives, cell phones, offices, desks, documents, mailroom, employees).

3. *Quantify the value of that data to your business.* Until you know what it is worth, you won't be willing to protect it accordingly. To estimate the value of your data, apply a value of $204[3] to every customer record and every employee record you collect, store, or transmit in any way. This is

the average cost per record of breach recovery. You will have to define internally the business-specific identity (e.g., intellectual property), according to your own formulas.

4. *Identify the three most vulnerable sources of potential theft.* For many businesses, the most common sources of theft are mobile data (laptops/smart phones), document storage/disposal, and insider theft. To maximize your ROI, focus on these areas first.

Results for the cost per data breach differ across industries, but according to the Ponemon Institute's Fifth Annual U.S. Cost of Data Breach Study, the cost to professional organizations is considerably higher than the overall average (see Figure 2.3). This suggests that these same organizations will realize an even higher ROI than the average. Now that we have defined the problem, we are ready to begin implementing the solution, which begins when we *engage the brain* in Chapter 3.

3 Engage the Brain

If protecting data privacy is presented in the same old technical and boring way, no one will listen or retain the knowledge long enough to put it to use.

Our task is to make data protection interesting and easy to remember. We must find a way to *engage the brain*. For attention and memory's sake, we *almost want to make a game out of security*, but without diminishing the seriousness of our task. Have you ever used a mnemonic device (usually in the form of a verbal memory aid) to help you remember the items on a test? A classic example is using the name Roy G. Biv to remember the colors of the rainbow (red, orange, yellow, green, blue, indigo, violet).

We are looking for a similar device to remind us of protecting our privacy, only more sophisticated. We want a way to think about and react to privacy in ways that are more natural to our current processes. We need a common language that connects privacy to something we already know and understand at an intuitive level. That is why I use the metaphor *thinking like a spy*.

Think Like a Spy

Let's say that your worst enemy is on a mission to steal everything you have— your private documents, home, investments, health, retirement, reputation, even your time. The only way that your enemy can steal these items is by spying on you, to exploit your vulnerabilities. Would that change the amount of information you give out, and to whom? Would it benefit you to understand the way that your enemy is thinking and spying on you?

I've just described the reality of identity theft and data breach. An enemy (dumpster diver, ruthless competitor, phisher, hacker, corporate spy, con artist, social engineer) is trying to steal your identity (your credit, savings, checking, investments, retirement, health insurance, reputation, and even who you are) by draining you and others of your private information. In many cases, the enemy is someone close to you, who steals from you to fund a gambling or drug habit or other dishonest endeavor.

Thinking like a spy is a paradigm, or a lens through which we see the world. This lens is designed to help you make a habit of privacy on a daily basis and recognize when your identity is at risk, personally or professionally. When identity is involved, we want to view the risk of losing it through the more critical "lens" of a spy. When it is not, we can put the lens away.

Know Thine Enemy

Why view identity through the eyes of a spy? We need to change our perspective because the old way (checklists, privacy policies, boring statistics) isn't getting the job done. Just as we can't remember the colors of the rainbow without a memory device, so we don't remember how to treat high-risk data unless we filter it through our new perspective. Spies are trained to have a heightened sense of awareness anytime they are in the field. Adopting this increased level of awareness will significantly help us to prevent identity theft. In its simplest form, thinking like a spy is nothing more than asking yourself: "What would my worst enemy do with this piece of information?"

Spies don't like to share their information. We must learn to be as defensive as they are when our personal information is on the table. This does not mean that we need to be paranoid. *Prevention is not about fear; fear is for people who take no action.* As our awareness, knowledge, and willingness to act increases, our fear will decrease. The spy mind-set will grow as we actively take steps to protect our privacy and expose less of our identity to danger. Once we have learned these techniques at a personal level, applying them at work becomes a natural response.

To summarize the ancient Chinese war strategist, Sun Tzu, author of *The Art of War: To defeat our enemies, we must be wise enough to learn from them.* A spy, unlike a simple thief, operates in two related worlds simultaneously: the world of information collection and the world of information protection. Spies go to great lengths and are well trained in protecting their real identities, as well as their aliases, informants, sources, agents, and network. From these skills, we can learn how to protect our sensitive information, whether it is physical (paper documents, credit cards, receipts), digital (laptops, e-mail, Internet, social networking, wireless transmissions), or human (what is in our brains). Spies are also masters of collecting information ("intelligence") on their subjects. This makes them uniquely qualified to serve as the lens through which we see how best to defend our privacy.

I have broken down our spy metaphor into seven distinct mind-sets that can be applied to almost any type of information privacy: at home and at work.

The Seven Mind-Sets of a Spy

The seven mind-sets of a spy, which I describe in greater detail in the respective chapter devoted to each (indicated in parentheses), are:

1. Eliminate the source (Chapter 4).
2. Destroy the data (Chapter 5).
3. Secure the systems (Chapter 6).
4. Lock the docs (Chapter 7).
5. Evaluate the risk (Chapter 8).
6. Interrogate the Enemy (Chapter 9).
7. Monitor the signs (Chapter 10).

Eliminate the Source

Spies eliminate unnecessary information at the source. For example, most spies are never told the end purpose of their missions, as it adds nothing to their effectiveness and minimizes leaks. Elimination takes place *before* the data is at risk. Applied to privacy, we can habitually eliminate exposed pieces of identity that are no longer necessary. By canceling an account we no longer use, we remove the risk of its theft. Inside organizations, eliminating unnecessary data collection, retention, mobility, and transmission can drastically reduce the risk of data breach.

Destroy the Data

Once it serves no further purpose, spies destroy all sensitive information. They use a device called a *burn box* that incinerates every last trace of data, physical or digital. Our gadgets are easier to come by, less expensive (shredders and digital shredding software), and serve the same purpose: to destroy anything containing private information that we no longer need.

Destroying takes place after data has been exposed, as opposed to elimination, which takes place before the data has been exposed. For example, when we are done with a bank statement, we should shred the document. In the office, we shred outdated personnel files, customer records, and extraneous documents containing intellectual capital, trade secrets, or company financials.

Secure the Systems

Secure technology has always been an important theme in the world of spies. Encryption, wire-tapping, listening bugs, hacking, and surveillance—these are all terms related to securing or compromising digital identity. As we continue to move our data online, *securing our digital assets will become the most important form of identity protection*. Whether it is a company laptop, your mobile phone, tape backups, wireless networking, or a server farm, technology houses vast quantities of data, making it an ideal target for theft.

> This chapter serves as a prerequisite to Chapter 12, "Defend Online Identity," and Chapter 13, "Protect Mobile Data," both found in Part III, "Field Combat: Target the Enemy," which covers protecting information on *social networking sites* (e.g., Facebook, YouTube, LinkedIn), information stored in the *cloud* (e.g., Google Docs, Hotmail, SalesForce), and mobile *data* (e.g., laptops, cell phones, thumb drives).

Lock the Docs

Any high-risk data assets that cannot be eliminated at the source, destroyed upon completion, or digitally secured must be locked up or effectively concealed. Locking is the default action when we need to keep information on hand, yet accessible to only certain individuals. *Lock the docs* refers to locking up paper documents such as passports, birth certificates, wills, deeds, trusts, financials, and other identity documents. In addition, *lock the docs* is meant to refer to *all types of identity that need to be physically locked up*, not just paper documents. Chapter 7 on this topic works in tandem with securing digital identity, as it is vital that digital data be physically locked, as well. For example, a laptop computer needs to be locked up physically (e.g., in the trunk of your car, office, hotel room—the most overlooked form of protection) and digitally (e.g., using passwords, security software, encryption, firewalls, etc.).

Evaluate the Risk

Spies have exceptional tools of observation, analysis, and evaluation that prepare them to preempt fraud at many levels. They are trained to detect fraud or social engineering (defined as the act of obtaining confidential information by manipulation) *before* they expose valuable intelligence. By learning to evaluate offers to share data, we arm ourselves against phishing and pharming schemes, financial scams, hacks, con jobs, and corporate espionage. Evaluation is a process of applying common sense and natural instinct to the constant barrage of information requests we receive. It establishes who we can trust, and how much. And it protects the most commonly exploited data leakage source of all: the *human source*.

Interrogate the Enemy

Spies ask direct and aggressive questions to get answers. This is an essential and foundational component of the *evaluation* process, described previously. Fostering an attitude of curiosity (and by extension into the corporate world, a culture of curiosity) is the *most powerful* critical thinking skill in your arsenal of information-protection tools. Employees who learn to think critically and ask the right questions regarding data privacy weave the fabric that makes up a Culture of Privacy.

Monitor the Signs

Spy networks monitor their assets (agents, information, safe houses) to detect trouble at the earliest stages. By monitoring indicators of breach or wrongdoing, they are able to contain information leakage before the damage becomes permanent. Correspondingly, by monitoring our identities (using either the latest technological tools or paper-based methods), we detect fraud and stop identity theft *before* it causes irrevocable damage. Tools you can use to keep track of your identity vital signs include:

- Identity theft monitoring services
- Credit report monitoring

- Balancing your checkbook
- Financial account alerts
- Social Security statement monitoring

At the organizational level, monitoring may include:

- Video surveillance
- Software footprint tracking
- Access log files
- Key card access tracking

The most powerful form of monitoring at the corporate level is actually performed by your customers.

Field Combat: Target the Enemy

Spies don't just learn in the classroom; they attain mastery by practicing what they have learned in the field. And so must you. The seven mind-sets just listed and discussed in Part II of the book don't exist in a vacuum; to be effective, they need to be combined and adapted to your lifestyle and your business. There is no silver bullet for protecting private information, but you will grow progressively safer as you adapt, prioritize, and accumulate individual levels of protection over months or years. Think of the process as securing your home with deadbolts, an alarm system, motion-sensitive lights, and a dog. Any one of these alone would be ineffective; but by layering security devices, your risk level begins to approach zero. The chapters in Part III, "Field Combat: Target the Enemy," apply the seven mind-sets in a more sophisticated, layered way to some of the highest-risk areas for identity theft and data breach.

Part III begins with four short, action-oriented chapters that serve as a bridge between the overlapping worlds of personal and professional privacy. They are:

Chapter 11 Deploy Targeting Strategies: Accumulate, Prioritize, and Adapt

This chapter gives a brief overview of *how* to target areas of risk. Spies don't operate "in theory"; they have to operate under the pressures applied by the real world. To survive, they learn to adapt to whatever threat faces them at the moment, to accumulate intelligence gradually, and to target the most valuable information first. We apply the same methods when targeting the enemies of data privacy.

Chapter 12 Defend Online Identity: Social Networking and the Cloud

We store massive amounts of information assets online, whether on social networking sites or more generally in the "cloud" (described fully in Chapter 6, "Secure the Systems"). It is no longer sufficient to *secure the systems*, which are mostly within our control. Those systems extend into the online world, far beyond our reach.

Chapter 13 Protect Mobile Data: Laptop Responsibility

Whether we are traveling across the city or around the globe, anytime data leaves our workspace, the risk of theft skyrockets. Protecting this information outside of the office will eliminate the single most damaging source of data theft in the workplace. This chapter takes a life-cycle look at protecting laptops, smart phones, and mobile computing devices.

Chapter 14 Travel with Care: Business Trips and Vacations

This chapter explains how travel heightens the risk of data theft. It combines a concentration of identity (e.g., mobile computing, travel documents, passports, itineraries, work files) with a somewhat unpredictable and unfamiliar environment (airports, hotels, taxi cabs, offices, conference rooms). Informed preparation is the key to safe travels.

Chapter 15 Recovering Your Identity: When All Else Fails

The second to last of the book, is for those who have already had their identities stolen. Hopefully, you will never need the information contained in this chapter.

Chapter 16 Prioritize Your Attack: The Privacy Calendar

The final chapter summarizes the book into a prioritized, step-by-step action item list for protecting your personal identity.

Basic Training: Think Like a Spy

[Identity] lies at the core of a great deal of what we do protecting our financial security, our personal security, and our reputational security. In the 21st Century, the most important asset that we have to protect as individuals and as part of our nation is the control of our identity, who we are, how we identify ourselves, whether other people are permitted to masquerade and pretend to be us, and thereby damage our livelihood, damage our assets, damage our reputation, damage our standing in the community.

—Michael Chertoff, U.S. Secretary of Homeland Security, August 2008, USC National Center for Risk Analysis of Terrorism Event

4

The First Mind-Set: Eliminate the Source

I dentity thieves target wallets, purses, laptops and carry-on luggage because they contain a high concentration of private information. The average purse contains 20 pieces of identity; the average smart phone or laptop, thousands.

Victim #9,437,988: Drop and Switch

Ashley wasn't a professional meeting planner, but due to layoffs, she had been forced to take on an additional role at her company: planning her industry association's largest event of the year. As a planner, Ashley had to travel. Between her laptop bag and purse, she carried a goldmine of identity while on the road, not all of it hers. In addition to her corporate-issued laptop and BlackBerry, she carried client files, her passport, driver's license, several credit cards, an insurance card, her Social Security card, and several pieces of vital information about her children.

Scheduled to fly to Orlando, Florida, one day before the conference began, Ashley arrived at the gate to discover that the last United Airlines flight to Florida had been cancelled. In a panic, she made her way to the customer service counter midway down the concourse. The long, winding line, at least 30 people deep, bottlenecked at the two exhausted agents on duty. When asked later by a policeman to describe the thief, she responded, in all seriousness, "I didn't see anything; it was like a teacher-less kindergarten room on

(continued)

(continued)

Halloween." At the time, she had exactly 14 hours before her first preconference event began.

While in line, Ashley had pulled her BlackBerry from her purse then set it down next to her laptop bag in order to free her hands to write. Focusing hard to hear the reservation agent who had found her an alternate airline and flight, Ashley barely paid attention when a woman put down her carry-on bag next to her own. As Ashley scribbled the new flight information on the back of her boarding pass, she never even noticed the woman picking up a handful of bags, including Ashley's. She did realize she no longer felt her bag leaning against her leg, but chose to ignore it—for only a split second.

The remains of Ashley's purse and bag were found in a women's restroom nearby. Her laptop, client files, and wallet were gone. Later, her driver's license and checkbook were used to purchase firearms at a traveling gun show. With her debit card, the thieves purchased ammunition from a Wal-Mart, which is also where they filled counterfeit prescriptions and billed them to her insurance company. To date, the gun has not been identified in a crime. Ashley spent approximately three months recovering her identity and her credit.

But the real devastation came from the loss of her company computer and client files, which were sold by the original thief to a more sophisticated crime ring. Because the computer had not been encrypted, and in accordance with the compliance laws in her state, Ashley's company was required to notify all affected individuals of a data breach. Her laptop contained the names, addresses, credit card numbers, and other undisclosed data on every one of the 5,700 conference attendees. It also contained sensitive intellectual capital about a pending merger and her employer's organization chart (which eventually led to the capture of one of the members of the crime ring when he tried to sell it to her company's largest competitor, who called the police).

Ashley made it to the conference, but later lost her job. Her company lost more than $4.1 million in lawsuits, victim recovery services, client defection, stock value, and legal fees. In contrast, the estimated cost to have trained Ashley on data privacy and to protect her laptop properly would have been approximately $194. The estimated cost to protect her entire company in the same way?: $45,000. Let's do the math to determine the return on privacy investment:

($4,100,000 − $45,000)/$45,000 = **9011%** Return on Privacy Investment

It is impractical to think that we can prevent our wallets, purses, computers, and mobile phones from ever being lost or stolen. To protect the identity and company information they hold, we need to minimize exposure across the board. We do this, at home and at work, by *eliminating the source.*

Eliminate Mind-Set

Spies carry as little sensitive information with them as possible, and spy networks systematically eliminate all potential sources of data leakage. In many cases, an agent knows only certain pieces of the information puzzle, making it nearly impossible to reconstruct the larger picture when a single piece falls into enemy hands.

By mirroring this process of elimination in our personal and professional lives, we minimize the quantity and quality of data we carry with us on a regular basis. It's not possible to lose what we don't have, and likewise impossible to steal what doesn't exist.

Ask yourself this simple question: What pieces of identity can I remove or *eliminate* (e.g., not carry it in my wallet, or store it in my filing cabinet, cell phone, or computer) before they cause me harm?

Spy networks operate on a need-to-know-basis. Spies are told no more than necessary, carry no more than necessary, and talk no more than necessary. Information is simplified because doing so makes it easier to track and keep safe. In addition, spies travel light. They carry no "incriminating" documents with them unless absolutely necessary.

The same should be true of your identity. The fewer pieces of personal information cluttering up your wallet, computer, filing cabinet, and brain (e.g., credit cards, bank accounts, brokerages, ID cards, passwords, etc.), the lower your statistical risk of loss or theft. The *elimination* mind-set suggests that if you don't need a particular piece of identity, get rid of it at the source. The source is whoever or whatever is generating the sensitive document.

This is a four-step process:

1. Eliminate your credit file as the number-one source of the most prevalent types of financial identity theft.
2. Begin eliminating every piece of plastic, paper, and electronic identity that you no longer use or need.

3. Reduce your online exposure by eliminating the buying and selling of your identity.
4. Eliminate the habit of signing up for new accounts unless they are absolutely necessary.

By keeping our identities simple, and sharing them only on a need-to-know basis, we have less to lose, less to be stolen, less to shred, less to lock up, and, consequently, more time and brain cells to protect items that we actually need.

Eliminate the Source

Source: Your Credit Report

Credit Freeze

If everyone in the country applied for a credit freeze, identity thieves would lose their major source of income. *A credit freeze is the single most significant and effective means of protecting your financial identity*, because it blocks almost everyone from setting up new forms of credit in your name. It is the equivalent of putting a password on your credit file.

> If you have been the victim of identity theft, don't freeze your credit *until the problem has been resolved.* It is very difficult to access your credit during the recovery process if it is already frozen.

While I recommend checking your credit report frequently for any signs of identity theft (see Chapter 10, "Monitor the Signs"), freezing your credit is a more proactive way to prevent theft before it happens and protect your credit information. The difference is similar to a house alarm being activated after thieves have broken in and done damage, versus installing on the doors deadbolt locks that cannot be broken and better secure the home.

Every time you establish new credit (e.g., open up a new credit card, store account, or bank account, or finance a car or apply for a home loan, etc.), an entry is created in your credit file, which is maintained by companies like Experian, Equifax, and TransUnion. The trouble is, with your name, address, and Social Security number in hand, an identity thief can pretend to be you and can establish credit (i.e., spend your net worth) in your name.

A credit freeze, also called a *security freeze*, is simply an agreement you make with the three main credit reporting bureaus (the aforementioned Experian, Equifax, and TransUnion). It means that they won't allow new accounts (credit card, banking, brokerage, loans, rental agreements, etc.) to be attached to your name/Social Security number unless you contact the credit bureaus, give them a password or PIN, and allow them to "unfreeze" or "thaw" your account for a short period of time.

This gives you control over who accesses your private information, and effectively prevents identity thieves from opening new accounts in your name. There is generally no charge to freeze your credit, though there may be a small fee to unfreeze it (see below). Note that you must contact each of the three credit reporting bureaus individually, as there is no way to freeze all three at once. The bureaus may require that requests be submitted by mail, so make sure that you use some form of package tracking to make sure they have been delivered. The bureaus will require the following information: your name, address, date of birth, Social Security number, copy of a valid ID, proof of address (e.g., copy of utility bill), as well as a copy of a police report if you have been the victim of identity theft.

The bureau will send you a letter confirming the freeze, and will include your PIN. Make sure you keep a record of your PIN in your dossier, as discussed in Chapter 10, "Monitor the Signs," for future reference. You definitely *do not* want to lose this number or have it fall into the wrong hands.

Temporarily reversing your credit freeze can be inconvenient, yes, but it serves as a reminder to keep your identity simple. You won't be signing up for any accounts that you don't absolutely need. To unfreeze your credit during a transaction (e.g., when you are applying for a car or home loan), you simply contact the credit bureaus (you are initiating the contact), give them your PIN, and ask them to temporarily unfreeze your credit. It costs about $10 anytime you want to unfreeze your report, and you can generally choose how long it remains unfrozen. Be sure to allow a couple of days to complete the transaction.

Many times the credit bureaus will recommend that you place a "fraud alert" on your credit file. Be aware that this alert lasts for only 90 days and is not always taken seriously, because many thieves know about it as well, and so may not try to use your stolen identity until after it expires. Also be aware that this process relies on businesses to properly check and confirm your identity. Unfortunately, businesses do not always perform the proper checks and so may unwittingly allow a thief to establish credit even when the fraud alert is in place. This makes freezing your credit the safest and most secure way to protect yourself.

However, by law, not all states allow you to freeze your credit, so the three credit reporting bureaus have begun to offer credit freezes on a national basis. Visit www.FinancialPrivacyNow.com for state-by-state details. You can also learn more at each individual credit bureau's website—though note that they frequently change their credit freeze addresses:

Equifax Security Freeze
P.O. Box 105788
Atlanta, Georgia 30348
Toll-Free: 1–800–685–1111
www.freeze.equifax.com/Freeze/jsp/SFF_PersonalIDInfo.jsp

TransUnion
Fraud Victim Assistance Department
P.O. Box 6790
Fullerton, CA 92834
Toll-Free: 1–888–909–8872
https://annualcreditreport.transunion.com/fa/securityFreeze/landing

Experian Security Freeze
P.O. Box 9554
Allen, TX 75013
Toll-Free: 1–888–397–3742
www.experian.com/freeze/center.html

Make sure you store your credit freeze documents in your dossier, as referred to earlier, so that you have easy access to them if you want to un-freeze your credit.

Source: Wallets and Purses

A lost or stolen wallet, purse, checkbook, or credit card accounts for a major portion of identity theft cases in which the victims knew how their identity was stolen.[1] That means we can protect a substantially large piece of the identity theft pie simply by safeguarding our wallets and purses. But this isn't always possible, so we must also learn how to minimize damage if it does fall into the wrong hands.

The more pieces of identity you *eliminate* from your wallet, the less susceptible you are to theft, and the easier it is to recover if you suddenly become a victim. Just as spies prepare themselves in case they fall into the hands of the enemy, you should be prepared to take action when your wallet or purse ends up in the hands of a criminal.

1. Remove the following items from your wallet or purse:

    Social Security Card (SSN): You only need this in rare circumstances (e.g., your first day on a new job). If stolen, it can be used to set up new credit card accounts, driver's licenses, loans, and bank accounts. It can also be used to steal your retirement benefits, draw unemployment, or file for bankruptcy. Your Social Security number is one of the pieces of your identity that you should protect most fiercely. File your card as discussed in Chapter 7, "Lock the Docs."

    Checks: Check fraud is one of the easiest forms of identity theft to carry out, hence one of the most prevalent. Stop carrying checks, and instead use your credit card or cash. Debit cards are not as safe, but they're better than checks. If you feel you can't survive without checks, carry them only when you go shopping, and make sure that your account has as little in it as possible (transfer any excess into your savings, until you need it). Don't make excuses for skipping this task, as doing so could have very negative consequences. Here is more specific advice:

    - *Know what thieves are after.* It is not just the physical check that the thief is looking for, but the account and bank routing numbers on the bottom of the check that allow the thief to make duplicate checks or access the account electronically, so carrying only one check in your purse or wallet isn't going to protect you much.

    - *Do not have your SSN, driver's license number, or home telephone number printed on your checks.* It is preferable to use a work address and phone number, which doesn't lead back to your home. Some people advise that you use your first and middle initials on the check, not your full name. This does a good job of concealing your name; the problem, however, is that most banks don't verify signatures on checks for less than $3,000 anyway, so taking this step probably won't stop fraud.

- *Never put full account numbers or Social Security numbers on the notes line of your check.* Use the last four digits *only*—banks and credit card companies can identify you from these numbers.
- *Always sign your checks (and vital documents) with a felt-tip or gel pen or permanent marker (like a Sharpie®).* This helps prevent thieves from "lifting" the ink from checks, mortgages, and other vital documents. I also recommend that you place a piece of clear plastic tape over the Pay To field so that it can't be easily changed. If a thief steals your check out of the mail and tries to tear off the tape to "wash" the Pay To field, it visibly damages the check and renders it void. If you make bank deposits by mail, I recommend using this same technique to protect the "For Deposit Only in Account XXX" line.

PIN Numbers and Passwords: Remove all passwords and PIN numbers from your purse or wallet for bank accounts, websites, debit cards, computers, home alarms, garage doors, and so on. Refer to Chapter 6, "Secure the Systems," for alternative ways to create and remember passwords so that you won't have to carry them with you.

Excess Credit and Debit Cards: We tend to accumulate credit cards and bank accounts even though we don't need them (usually because we received a short-term "bribe" for signing up). Remove them from your wallet; more, consider cancelling all of these excess accounts. Keep in mind, however, that when you cancel credit card accounts, it may lower your credit score, so check with your financial advisor before taking this step. One simple way to avoid negatively affecting your credit score is to lock up the extra card at home. If possible, carry no more than two cards in your wallet. This will make posttheft recovery much easier and less time-consuming.

Credit Card Receipts: File receipts securely if you need them for tax purposes or expense tracking. Otherwise, destroy them. To learn about how best to destroy documents, credit cards, CD-ROMs, and other forms of identity, go to Chapter 5, "Destroy the Data." And to find more information on what to lock up and how to secure your documents, read Chapter 7, "Lock the Docs."

ATM Receipts and Bank Deposit Slips: Record the transactions and shred them once they have cleared your bank.

2. Remove your Social Security number from any identification cards:

   Driver's License: In some states, SSNs still appear on your driver's license. Most states will allow you to remove it from your card, but doing so may require getting a new driver's license. It is worth the trouble.

   Medical Cards: SSNs are still occasionally printed on medical insurance or HMO/PPO cards. In many states, the insurance company is required to send you a new card with a non-SSN identification number, if requested. Make the request. Medicare/Medicaid cards use Social Security numbers, so carry them only when necessary.

   Student ID Cards: Some colleges and universities use your SSN as a student ID number. Request a new card with a different method of identification.

   Military ID/Government Cards: Many government-issued cards use your SSN for identification. Some branches of the military require you to carry your card at all times, in which case you are out of luck. Check with your specific agency or branch to find out if you must carry your card at all times. Otherwise, carry it only when necessary. Fortunately, the military is actively working to remove SSNs from ID cards.

3. Take these precautions in case your wallet is stolen:

   Use Both Signature and "Photo ID Required": Sign your credit cards with *both* your signature and "Photo ID Required." Also, write the same message on the front of the card with indelible ink (since most stores don't even look at your signature on the back). Though it can be removed somewhat easily, it helps to discourage thieves, as you are sending the message that you are watching out for identity theft. *Be aware that you need to sign your name on the back of the card to be in compliance with many credit card company contracts.* Without your signature, some of them can deny any claims of fraud and refuse to reimburse what was stolen. Don't simply write "Photo ID Required."

   Photocopy: Make a photocopy (front and back) of *every piece of identity* that you keep in your wallet. If it is lost or stolen, this will make it easy to call the companies and cancel your cards, accounts, and so on. File the copy in your dossier, as discussed in Chapter 10, "Monitor the Signs."

4. Consider additional protection measures:

   Rotate Credit Cards: If you have been a victim of data loss (where your private data has been lost or stolen from a major corporation, as happened recently at Heartland Payment Systems) or just want to "outdate" your credit card identity, once a year cancel the cards you do keep. Call each credit card company, cancel your existing card, and have the firm issue a new card with a new credit card number. This means that all of those companies that have your credit card on file now have old data. By opting out of a great deal of information sharing (described in the next section), your new card number won't be in as many databases. Don't forget to:

- Have any frequent-flyer miles transferred to your new card number, or have your frequent-flyer number attached to the new card. You don't want to lose miles just because you are being diligent about your identity.

- Call any companies that have your credit card number on file for auto-pay (phone bill, electricity, etc.) and let them know your new number. Anyone who tries to use the old number will draw blanks. This measure isn't to protect against money loss (you only have a $50 liability on any credit card if you report it as lost or stolen in the company's "acceptable" time frame); it's to protect against having to spend extra time if your credit card number is stolen.

Pay with Cash: This old-fashioned way of paying incurs absolutely zero identity "creep." Pay with cash when you don't want to let your card out of your sight or don't want to share information that will ultimately be stored in a database and sold to other businesses. Companies buy your credit card histories so they can market other services to you. For example, certain businesses know that if you shop at a particular store, you are likely to buy their product.

From today on, make your wallet a sacred place. Don't add identity information to it unless it is absolutely necessary. Use it as a control point to stop identity creep (slow and unnecessary leakage of our personal information). Lock it up at the gym (in private) and don't leave it exposed in your car or at work. Finally, don't forget to have your spouse or partner and other family members follow the same steps.

Source: Junk Mail, Telemarketing, and Information Commerce

Your personal information is collected, sold, and resold. It is generally used to determine credit risk, and marketing departments use it to sell items to you.

The more you *eliminate* this buying and selling of your private data, the lower your risk becomes. As you learn of companies and organizations that collect your data, *opt out* of their information sharing. You opt out by calling the number on your statements or cards and asking the respective companies about their privacy policies. If they are written in legal gibberish, tell them that you don't want your personal information to be shared with anyone (including other subsidiaries of the same company). Ask to be removed from all junk mail and marketing lists, telemarketing lists, and any other form of marketing campaigns. Tell them to stop sending "convenience checks," "courtesy checks," preapproved credit cards, or any other form of credit.

As you start to "go undercover," you will begin reducing the quantity of information you share within and between companies. This lowers your chances of identity theft, and saves you time opening and shredding useless but potentially dangerous mail.

In this section, I list a handful of places to opt out. Contact one or two a day for the next few weeks and you will start to see your junk mail and telemarketing calls diminish. Alternatively, follow the instructions I give in Chapter 16, "Prioritize Your Attack: The Privacy Calendar," and you will have opted out of these lists after only a month.

Many of the opt-out addresses change frequently (possibly so that people have a harder time taking this protective step), so if the links given here are no longer working, or you would like a centralized place for all opt-out websites, please visit www.Sileo.com/opt-out.

Credit Offers: Opt out of prescreened credit offers, which are frequently stolen from mailboxes. Prescreened credit offers are sent after companies have checked your credit history with one of the three credit bureaus (Equifax, Experian, or TransUnion) and offer you more credit based on your good credit history. This could be a preapproved credit card, loan, or line of credit. Call 1-888-5OPTOUT (1–888–567–8688), or visit www.OptOutPreScreen.com. Because your credit is preapproved on these offers, it is a very attractive target for an identity thief.

Credit Cards: For each credit card that you haven't cancelled, contact the issuer and tell the customer service representative that you wish to opt out of all information sharing, both within the company and with other companies. And while you have the CSR on the phone:

- Direct the company to stop sending you convenience checks (which are frequently stolen from mail boxes), marketing e-mails, and telemarketing calls. Ask whom else you need to contact within the company to get off *all* lists.
- Ask if you can receive your statements by e-mail only, as the paper versions are another item routinely stolen from unlocked mailboxes. If you aren't comfortable using a computer to receive statements, or don't have a computer, you will learn in Chapter 7, "Lock the Docs," other methods for protecting your mail. It is important to make the *seven mind-sets of prevention* work within your lifestyle, as that is the only practical way that you will follow through on the changes.

Financial Institutions: Contact your insurance companies, brokerages, banks, and any other financial institutions to opt out of all information sharing. Switch to receiving online statements wherever possible. As the paper statements arrive from each of these institutions, make the changes.

Telemarketing: Place your name on the National Do Not Call Registry. This will cut down considerably on telemarketing calls. Visit www.DoNotCall.gov and fill out the form for adding your phone numbers (home, cell, business, spouse's/family members' cells).

Although most states have discontinued their individual do not call registries, find out whether your state still maintains a separate list where you can register your phone number. For more information on where to contact in your state, visit www.the-dma.org/government/donotcalllists.shtml. Don't forget to add any home phone numbers, as well as cell phones, business phones, and your spouse or partner's and family members' cell phones.

Junk Mail: Remove your name from the Direct Marketing Association's mailing list. This will cut down on the majority of your junk mail. To learn more, visit www.DMAChoice.org and fill out the form for removing your name. It costs $1 whether you register online or through the mail. Don't forget to remove your spouse's/partner's and other family members' names, as well.

While at this site, you can learn more about the types of marketing mail sent to you and how to opt out of the majority of it that you receive. The site allows you to "customize your mailbox" and eliminate any source of marketing mail that you no longer want to receive. Once you indicate you do not want to receive *any* type of junk mail, companies are required to remove you from their direct mailing lists.

Directories: Delete your phone number from Google's reverse directory. To see if your number is listed, go to www.google.com and type your phone number into the search window. If it comes up with your name or address, you're listed! Visit www.google.com/help/pbremoval.html and fill out the form to have your information removed. Similarly, remove your personal information from Zabasearch. To see if your personal information is listed there, go to www.zabasearch.com and type your name into the search window. If it comes up with your name or address, you're listed! E-mail info@zabasearch.com with your full name and address to have your information removed. The site will answer back with a list of options that you can take.

There are many websites like Zabasearch that aggregate data and offer it for sale. Other examples are whitepages.com, intelius.com, pipl .com, anywho.com, peoplefinder.com, people.yahoo.com, and findsomeone.com. Removing your identity from these sites may seem like a futile effort because new aggregators pop up constantly; therefore, I recommend this step only for people who are very aggressive about their efforts to eliminate exposure of their information.

The key is to remove your name from each search engine as you hear about it. Start by searching for your full name in Google. For most people, this will bring up all possible "people search engines" where you are listed. Once you have obtained this list, e-mail each individual search engine to have your name removed. In many cases you will be required to "snail-mail" the request (to discourage people from doing it). Make sure you mail safely. Request a confirmation of removal so that you can hold the sites accountable, if necessary.

White Pages: Call your local phone company and ask to have your phone number delisted when the next edition of the White Pages is published. You can also go to yellowpages.com and click on Find A Person. Enter your information to search for yourself and, if your listing comes up, click on Remove Listing below. This is where many mailing list companies collect data and sell it to other companies.

Discounts and Contests: Learn to say no. Stop signing up for new credit cards, checking accounts, contests, discount cards, even if the "bribe" is appealing. The amount of time you will save by keeping your identity more private and by eliminating hours opening junk mail will more than surpass the enticement you were being offered.

Warranty Cards: Stop filling out warranty registration cards unless it is necessary to enact the warranty (it rarely is). Warranty cards are generally used by the company's marketing department, which sells your information to other businesses or attempts to sell you related items. They often request a great deal of personal information that has nothing to do with the warranty.

Surveys: Stop completing surveys, unless they are anonymous or very important to you. Check the back of "anonymous" surveys for a small barcode that links the survey to your identity.

Source: Your Mail

The more mail you stop, junk or legitimate, the less chance it will be stolen. Mail theft is easy and very productive for identity thieves, especially when you don't have a locking box.

Not only is minimizing the mail you receive an easy way to simplify your identity, it also serves as an excellent way to accumulate change—as long as you act on mail items as soon as they arrive. Here's how:

1. *Receive statements online.* Every time a piece of legitimate mail (credit card, bank, insurance, telephone, energy, water, and sewage statements, mileage points, etc.) arrives over the next few months, call the company (you'll find the customer service number on the statement) and ask to receive your statement online. Thereafter, review and store your statements on your computer, if possible; doing so is much safer than receiving these documents through the mail and storing them in a filing cabinet. If you don't use a computer, read the section on securing your mail in Chapter 7, "Lock the Docs."

2. *Simplify your mail.* For each account you have, ask yourself how much you use it, to determine if you absolutely need to keep it active. If you no longer use the account, cancel it, just as you did for your wallet items. If you miss one, catch it next month. This is the beauty of accumulating change (as discussed in Chapter 11, "Deploy Targeting Strategies: Accumulate, Prioritize, and Adapt"): it doesn't have to occur in one day.

Because paper trails tend to be the most easily accessible source of private information, avoiding the use of paper bills and banking statements altogether is a surefire way to eliminate paper-based theft.

—"2009 Identity Fraud Report," Javelin Strategy & Research

Source: Cell Phones

Cell phones and digital assistants carry a treasure trove of information. They often have passwords, Social Security numbers, bank account numbers, birthdates, addresses, and phone numbers stored in them (for you and all of your contacts). To protect those valuable identity items, follow these guidelines:

Passwords

Most cell phones (especially smart phones like iPhones and BlackBerrys) have password protection. This simple step goes a long way toward protecting the data on your phone and preventing a criminal from making calls on your dollar. If nothing else, it slows down the thief long enough to have your data remotely "wiped" or eliminated. Currently, many cell phones (like the iPhone) allow you to log in to your phone from your computer and remotely erase all data on the device, even if someone else has possession of it. Then, when you get a new phone, you simply sync it to your computer and, voila, your data is on your new handset.

- If you can't lock your phone, use the password suggestions in Chapter 6, "Secure the Systems," to conceal passwords and private information.
- If you have no way to protect the data in your cell phone, take private information out of it.

Source: Website Data Leakage

Websites

When you are on an Internet site that offers you free content in exchange for your personal information (e.g., newspapers, music downloads, and web support), think twice before making the trade. Is the content really worth it? If so, provide as little data as required to get the benefit; also see if the site will accept generic data (e.g., John Doe, 123 Main St . . .). If you want to avoid future spam (discussed next), give a fake e-mail address, like abc@def.com. If, however, the site requires a confirmation e-mail (one you have to open and respond to), you will need to provide a legitimate address. Keep in mind, the simpler you keep your response, the less identity you will have floating on the Internet.

Make sure that the Internet sites that you visit regularly have your current address and phone number. You don't want these companies sending statements or other information to an outdated address.

Spam

Set up a free e-mail account (e.g., on Gmail, Hotmail, or Yahoo! Mail) to use when you don't want to reveal your permanent or professional e-mail account. When setting these up, make sure that you opt out of all shared information; and, again, give as little personal data as possible. When you start receiving too much spam on this account, simply shut it down and register a new, clean e-mail address.

Source: Your Car

Remove all identity documents out of your glove compartment. Ideally, lock these documents up. If this is not practical, move your proof of insurance and car registration to an out-of-the-way, unlikely place, but one that is easy for you to remember, such as an Altoids or Band-Aid canister that fits in the compartment between the front seats. Thieves who break into cars generally have to work so quickly that they won't take the extra time to search for documents that aren't in the obvious places—in the glove compartment or behind a visor.

For even greater protection, buy an AutoSafe, such as those sold by SentrySafe, and lock your sensitive documents in there, and store the safe in the trunk of your car. You can also store your computer hard drive or any other valuables in the safe when you are traveling. If you get pulled over, explain to the police officer *before* you get out of the car why you keep your information in the trunk.

Lock your car repair and oil change receipts in your home filing cabinet. You generally need these items only when you are selling or have a problem with your car. They do not need to be in the car itself.

Action Item Checklist: Eliminate the Source

☐ Freeze your credit with Equifax, Experian, and TransUnion.
☐ Remove the following items from your wallet or purse:
  - Social Security card
  - Checks
  - PIN numbers and passwords
  - Excess credit and debit cards
  - Credit card receipts
  - ATM receipts and bank deposit slips
☐ Remove your Social Security number (SSN) from any identification cards.
☐ Sign credit cards and include "Photo ID Required."
☐ Photocopy every piece of identity in your wallet, and store the copies safely.
☐ Opt out of information sharing, telemarketing, and junk mail.
☐ Place your name on the National Do Not Call Registry.
☐ Remove your name from physical and online directories.
☐ Reduce incoming paper mail and switch to e-mail statements.
☐ Password-protect your cell phone (and PDA).
☐ Reduce unnecessary Internet accounts and website access.
☐ Eliminate all identity documents from your car, or lock them up in it.

For a complete, prioritized list of all of the action steps you can take to protect yourself, read Chapter 16, "Prioritize Your Attack: The Privacy Calendar."

Business Relevance

Avoiding mistakes is one of those unseen, unheralded achievements that are not allowed to take up our time and thought. And yet . . . many times, avoiding a bad deal can affect the bottom line more significantly than scoring a big sale. . . . That's the funny thing
(continued)

(*continued*)
about stopping some behavior. It gets no attention, but it can be as crucial as everything else we do combined.

—Marshall Goldsmith,
What Got You Here Won't Get You There (pp. 36–37)

Eliminating the source plays a vital role in protecting corporate data, just as it does in protecting your personal information. In business, eliminating the source is not only a tactical procedure (e.g., stop carrying sensitive customer information on your laptop), it is also a strategic initiative, one that prompts us to look at internal behaviors leading to unsafe data. There are a handful of bad habits regarding data handling that, when *eliminated*, will make it substantially easier to implement a Culture of Privacy.

Take a few moments to think about how your organization can best eliminate the seven deadly sins of data privacy:

1. *Apathy:* Apathy is a disturbing lack of care about and attention to a crime you incorrectly believe will never seriously impact your bottom line. If you have never had a corporatewide privacy education initiative, you are a prime candidate for this weakness.
2. *Ignorance:* Many leaders refuse to admit that they don't know what they don't know. For example, do you know the value, location, and confidentiality level of your firm's sensitive data? Do you know how it is protected, how long it is maintained, and why it is kept in the first place?
3. *Arrogance:* Some executives see themselves as champions of data privacy because they have a strong IT department, but fail to recognize that privacy doesn't exist in a silo. Does your organization tend to believe that data privacy is the realm of the IT department? If so, you are overlooking other critical functions (human resources, sales, intellectual property, legal compliance, facilities maintenance) that are touched by privacy concerns on a daily basis.
4. *Greed:* External profit pressures are so strong on most corporations that leadership can't see the forest for the trees. What percentage of your profits goes toward protecting your information assets? If you don't know, you are at risk.

5. *Hypocrisy:* Many CEOs are the first to violate the very privacy policies that they champion. Have you ever surfed unprotected at the airport? Do you shred every piece of sensitive data that goes in your trash? What passwords are stored in your BlackBerry?

6. *Paralysis:* Some companies and executives have difficulty breaking old habits and, by default, choose to perpetuate high-risk data practices. Do you collect certain private information simply because you always have? Have you ever reevaluated your hiring policies to take into account corporate espionage, workplace identity theft, and insider fraud?

7. *Procrastination:* Even some executives who care about, educate themselves on, admit to, have the budget to invest in, and personally practice data safety never get around to addressing it at the corporate level. When you are finished reading this book, do you think your behavior will change? Or will you still say, "I'll get to it later?"

This is not an easy topic, but running an organization isn't an easy task. Leaders who guide their corporations to develop a privacy strategy that *eliminates* these security sins will achieve a long-term competitive advantage in the marketplace.

5

The Second Mind-Set: Destroy the Data

Sometimes the people picking up your garbage don't think of it as trash; they think of it as cash. And sometimes the trash man is really a "broker," selling bags of trash to the highest bidder. With such a high percentage of identity theft being committed using traditional methods (e.g., physical document theft), destroying paperwork you don't use or need is an essential step to take to prevent data breach.

Victim #2,010,336: The Cash Men

The Donaldsons had just purchased a new home. They closed on the house on Thursday, removed the "For Sale" sign on Friday, and moved in over the weekend. The following Wednesday was their trash pickup day, and by then, they had plenty of it.

The garbage was picked up while they were at work. They assumed it had all been taken by the waste and recycling company. They were wrong. Little did they know that by removing the "For Sale" sign, they had inadvertently sent a signal to a local identity theft crime ring (referred to as the Cash Men, a play on "trash men") to pay attention. The thieves had learned that the trash of new homeowners often is, for several weeks, a good source of copies of financial documents. These docs typically contain every piece of identity a thief wants and needs—Social Security numbers, birthdates, addresses, phone numbers, bank accounts—and all available for pickup from one convenient location.

To avoid looking suspicious, the Cash Men used a standard-looking trash truck to pick up select bags of information throughout the neighborhood. After finding what they wanted in the Donaldson's trash, the thieves promptly submitted a false change of address that routed the family's mail to an untraceable post office box. By first "washing" checks and then applying for new credit cards with one of the Social Security numbers they found, the Cash Men were able to take out a loan to fund a full-scale methamphetamine lab.

The Cash Men were fully aware that because the Donaldsons had just made a major purchase (the house), they probably wouldn't be applying for credit any time soon—which is when most people discover identity theft. And they were right. It was 23 months and tens of thousands of dollars later when the Donaldsons found out, and in the worst circumstance possible: when the police showed up to arrest them for running a meth lab.

All because they had failed to purchase and use a $100 document shredder.

Destroy Mind-Set

Spies cover their tracks by destroying the paper trail. When they no longer need a piece of physical information, they throw it in a "burn bag," where it is incinerated.

We must follow their lead and systematically destroy any private information that could lead to identity theft, if it were to fall into the wrong hands. We do this by using document shredders, on-site shredding, and digital shredding.

Every act of creation is first an act of destruction.

—Pablo Picasso

Identity thieves are experts at collecting data that is not properly destroyed. They generally do this by digging through your trash ("dumpster diving") on the curbside or in a company dumpster. In some cases, this is even legal, as trash is not necessarily considered private property once it passes through your front door.[1] Thieves also pick up credit card receipts on restaurant tables once the guests have left and before the waiter has collected them. Sometimes, the waiter is the thief. Few people realize that credit card "masking" (covering up all of the numbers except the last four) is required by law *only* on the customer's copy of the receipt, not the merchant copy. That means the merchant copy often contains your entire credit card number.

To increase your safety, you need to destroy historical records (old bank statements, tax records, cancelled checks, computer files, etc.), as well as current documents that would otherwise go out in the trash. The simple rule of thumb is: *Destroy* anything with a piece of identity on it that will be thrown out with the trash, left in someone else's control, or can't be locked up.

Once you put your identity in someone else's hands (the people who clean your office, the garbage man, the waiter, the sales clerk), your risk of identity theft immediately escalates. This should trigger alarms and cause you to think twice about releasing your information from your control. Use this rule of thumb when you are uncertain of what to destroy: When in doubt, *destroy* it. There are very few documents that can't be re-created.

Destroy Physical Information: Files, Documents, Credit Cards

A paper shredder is the best means of destroying documents, disks, and credit cards. Tearing documents into small pieces is *not* sufficient, as it simply signals to thieves which pieces of trash are worth reconstructing. Choosing which documents to keep and which to destroy is a personal choice, and it can be a difficult one to make. To help make these decisions, keep in mind that the more you destroy, the less you will need to secure (see Chapter 7, "Lock the Docs").

In terms of shredding, *convenience is everything!* Place the shredder near to where you open mail or file documents, so that you will remember to shred what you would otherwise automatically throw away. If there are several locations throughout your home where you keep papers, make it a practice to collect them from each location and shred them once or twice a week before they go into the trash. For even better results, buy a shredder for each location where you handle sensitive information. The easier it is to shred, the more likely you will do it.

One word of caution: Make sure to place the shredder out of reach of small children; better yet, purchase a shredder that automatically shuts down when small fingers or pets get too close (I use Fellowes' SafeSense™ shredders).

Review the table here for an idea of what a thief can find *just* in your mailbox, and how it can be used to steal your identity.

Piece of Mail	What It Contains	How It Is Used
Credit card statements	Your name, address, creditor's name, account number, and details	Make online purchases; change the address where statements are sent
Paycheck stubs	Your name, pay rate, employer details, and maybe even your Social Security number	To apply for new credit and other accounts (especially powerful with your Social Security number)
New checks	Your name, address, bank's name, account number, routing number, possibly phone number, or Social Security number	Write checks in your name and access the money in your bank account
Bank statements	Your name, address, bank's name, account number, and balance	Access your bank records and the money in your bank accounts
Investment and brokerage statements	Your name, address, account number, balance, account manager, Social Security number	Cash out your investments, or any of the crimes above
Preapproved credit card offers	Your name, address, and the offer	Apply for a credit card in your name, but sent to an anonymous address
Utility and phone bills	Your name, address, account number	Set up service in thief's name, with you still listed as person paying the bills
Convenience checks	Your name, address, account number, and balance	Write and cash checks in your name and access your credit card account

For a more comprehensive list of items that end up in the trash, refer back to Chapter 2, "Define the Problem." Also examine the table in Chapter 7, "Lock the Docs," for suggestions on which documents to lock up.

The best way to determine which historical financial documents to destroy is to ask your tax accountant and/or lawyer. You will be well served to learn from an expert in your area who is familiar with your needs. When this isn't possible, lock up the documents rather than destroying them.

Destroy Physical Information

The most important piece of advice I can give in regard to this important piece of equipment is to *purchase a high-quality document shredder*. Go to your local office supply store, or visit www.Sileo.com/productreviews for our reviews on the best shredders. I recommend you choose one with the following features:

- Cross-cut confetti shredding that shreds in increments smaller than two inches. Strip shredders make it too easy to reconstruct documents, and often leave account numbers intact along one of the strips.
- Has a simultaneous feeding capacity of 10-plus pages. If the shredder takes fewer sheets than 10 at a time, you are more likely to grow impatient with how long it takes to destroy documents, and give up.
- Allows shredding of stapled documents, CD-ROMs, and credit cards.
- Has jam-proof technology, to prevent you from overloading the shredding mechanism.

Start shredding any papers that are going in the trash immediately. Be generous with what you shred—overcompensating won't hurt you (unless of course you shred something you need, which is why you need to first consult with an expert). For added security, throw the cut-up or broken sections of credit cards into separate loads of trash to make it impossible to reconstruct them.

As you file your latest statements, cancelled checks, tax information, and so on, decide whether it is time to destroy outdated copies of these documents. Consult with your accountant first, to ensure that you know what to keep for tax purposes or other reasons.

Use your new shredder as the motivation to clean off the piles of identity on your desk, in your files, and throughout the house.

Thirteen percent of identity theft is committed by someone the victim knows. This number rises to 31 percent among low-income consumers, who are the most severely impacted victims because they are less likely to be notified of data breach than the average.

—*"2009 Identity Fraud Survey Report" (pp. 46, 75), Javelin Strategy & Research*

Domestic help, contract workers, guests, and even friends and family often commit identity theft inside of the home. By shredding and locking all sensitive documents, you lessen the temptation and opportunity for dishonest visitors.

When you are in a restaurant or retail store, scratch out all but the last four digits on the merchant copy of your credit card receipt (as I noted previously, the law allows merchants to maintain it on their copy of the receipt, but they no longer need it once the transaction has been processed). Tear up your copy if you don't need it for your records. Likewise, tear up any carbon paper if the merchant uses manual-swipe receipts.

Destroy Digital Information: Disks, E-mails, CDs

One of the main reasons we destroy old paper files is because they take up space, which can be expensive, especially if you lock them up. With computer files, this is less of an issue. As long as your computer is well protected (see Chapter 6, "Secure the Systems") and has enough storage space (a large hard drive), you gain less by deleting documents from your computer. If you want to clean files off for the sake of organization, I recommend copying them onto a CD or DVD disk that you protect with passwords or encryption (more complex) or store in your fire safe (easier). This is one of the many factors that make a computer such a good tool for preventing identity theft. By taking some basic measures, you can lock down your system (and therefore your identity) without going to great lengths. I discuss this further in Chapter 6.

There are, however, a couple of exceptions. First, if you are donating or throwing away a computer, you should electronically "shred" the hard drive before you pass it on. This can be done using any number of programs or by performing a low-level format on the hard drive. I recommend leaving this to a computer technician, as it is a permanent and unrecoverable means of destruction. The data on your computer may be worth thousands of dollars, so having it professionally deleted or transferred to another computer is a good investment. And if you have a notebook computer, I recommend adding a second level of protection, called *encryption*. See Chapter 6 for details.

Before selling or donating your computer, make sure you have formatted the hard drive so that your data cannot be reconstructed. Similarly, if you are throwing away or selling a cell phone, be sure to reformat the memory card before you do so.

Action Item Checklist: Destroy the Data

☐ Purchase a high-quality, confetti document shredder, and shred every document, disk, and credit card that you no longer need.
☐ Scratch out all but the last four digits on merchants' copies of your credit card receipt (if they don't mask it).
☐ Before selling, donating, or passing on your computer or cell phone to someone else, have it digitally shredded or low-level formatted.

Here is a quick list of some of the most vulnerable items that go out in the trash, hence are good candidates for the shredder once you no longer need them (consult with your accountant or attorney):

☐ Preapproved credit card offers
☐ Convenience checks from credit card companies
☐ Copies of mortgage and loan documents
☐ Credit card statements
☐ Cancelled checks
☐ Bank statements
☐ Credit card receipts
☐ Pay stubs
☐ Utility bills
☐ Phone bills
☐ Cell phone bills
☐ Insurance/medical statements
☐ Car registration/insurance
☐ Brokerage statements
☐ Copies of tax records or notes that are no longer needed
☐ Expired driver's licenses
☐ Expired credit cards

Business Relevance

For businesses, shredding is low-hanging fruit (one of the easiest sources of data breach to eliminate). But businesses are so often focused on electronic forms of data breach that they fail to heed the following statistics highlighted in a recent Ponemon Institute study[2] conducted for the Alliance for Secure Business Information:

- More than 50 percent of sensitive business data is still stored on paper documents.
- Forty-nine percent of data breaches reported in the survey were the result of paper documents.
- Sixty percent of businesses admitted that they didn't provide the proper tools (e.g., shredders) to safely discard documents that were no longer needed.
- The average data breach recovery cost according to this survey was $6.3 million.

If you own a business, make sure to destroy sensitive documents prior to discarding them, to decrease your legal liability. Businesses are required to destroy all consumer information before discarding it in the trash. The Fair & Accurate Credit Transaction Act (FACTA) Disposal Rule states that "any person who maintains or otherwise possesses consumer information for a business purpose" must properly destroy the information prior to disposal. FACTA further states that every person and/or business must take "reasonable measures" to protect against unauthorized access to the use of the information in connection with its disposal. The Red Flags Rules dictated by the Federal Trade Commission raise this standard even higher.

Here are a few document-shredding best practices to implement at your organization:

- Provide employees with a *list of common documents* they should be shredding.
- As in the home, when it comes to shredding, *convenience is key*. Adhere to the three-second rule: If your employees can't shred a

(continued)

(continued)

document within three seconds, the shredder is too far away to encourage consistent shredding.

- For highest security, place a shredder *at every workstation*, as well as near any photocopiers, printers, or common areas where documents are handled.
- Purchase *high-quality shredders* that won't break down, that prevent employees from overfeeding the shredder, and that warn you when they need to be oiled or maintained.
- Resort to on-site truck shredders and locked shredding bins *only when you have massive quantities* of shredding to complete (e.g., when you are purging historical archives). I don't recommend bulk shredding for everyday use because there are too many ways for the data to be compromised before it is destroyed (e.g., the shredding bins are broken into; the shredding company does not properly destroy or dispose of the documents).
- *Train company executives* to take shredding very seriously and to become high-profile users of the shredders (to set a positive example).

6

The Third Mind-Set: Secure the Systems

I n the very near future, digital identity theft will become more common than identity theft via paper documents, stolen wallets, and dumpster divers. Because of the vast quantities of data we store digitally (on computers, cell phones, in the "cloud," on thumb drives, etc.), it is becoming more cost-effective for thieves to take control of one hard drive than 100 filing cabinets.

Victim #4,900,003: Facebook Company Identity Theft

As the bookkeeper for an Internet wine retailer, Gregg had access to nearly every digital file, filing cabinet, and financial record in the corporation. If someone in the company needed data, he had it. Gregg didn't spend much time on social networking sites like Facebook during working hours because his boss, Stefanie, was said to have installed software surveillance on everyone's system to monitor how much work time they were spending on personal matters. But he made an exception when he received an e-mail from Facebook titled "Facebook Password Reset Confirmation," which asked him to log in to his account directly ("for security purposes—never click on a link in an e-mail," it said) where he read the full notification in his Facebook inbox. Because the warning mirrored the company's established security procedure (don't click on links in e-mails; log in directly), he assumed it was legitimate.

(continued)

(continued)

And since he managed the company's Facebook page, which had thousands of wine-enthusiast fans, he wanted to make sure its profile was online.

He logged in to Facebook and read the message in his inbox, which asked him to click on a link that would verify his login credentials. If he didn't update his login information quickly, it warned, he would be locked out of his account. Because it wasn't from a financial institution (or eBay or PayPal) and because it was in his Facebook inbox, Gregg didn't think twice or consider that it could be a phishing scam set up to capture his login name and password. When he clicked on the link, it took him to a login page identical to the one he had just left, so he reentered his information. There he noticed that the URL address in the address bar had changed, but it still contained the words "Facebook" and "login" as part of the address, so once again, he assumed it was legitimate.

It wasn't.

The minute he clicked on the link, a variant of the Bredolab Trojan horse (described below) began downloading onto his computer. Because his antivirus and antispyware software hadn't yet been updated for Bredolab, the Trojan went undetected. By the time Gregg had finished retyping his login name and password (which gave the thieves full access into his Facebook account), the Trojan had already gone to work. By injecting its own programming code into otherwise legitimate Windows processes, the Trojan:

1. *Bypassed the corporate firewall (allowing restricted private data to be sent out of the office);*
2. *Completely turned off all virus and malware monitoring (so that the Trojan could operate in stealth mode, unable to be detected by security software); and*
3. *Enabled a "bot," which immediately began spamming more "Facebook Password Reset Confirmation" e-mails to everyone on the company's Facebook address list. This is a particularly dangerous and viral way for the scam to propagate, as people tend to trust messages from their "friends" on Facebook.*

In less than 30 seconds, Gregg had lost access to his Facebook account, control of his hard drive, and ownership of his wine-enthusiast list.

The Bredolab Trojan is a banking parasite, meaning that it searches for online banking information stored on its host's computer. In this case, the bank account numbers stored on Gregg's computer were company accounts, not personal. Nevertheless, Gregg was still the first to know that the accounts had been cleaned out when he received an automatic e-mail alerting him to the account activity. Gregg had unfortunately stored the company's checking and savings account numbers and password in his Outlook address book.

After changing the password so that Gregg could no longer access the Facebook account, the thieves began e-mailing his competitors to see if they wanted to purchase his customer list. This wasn't just a listing of Facebook fans, but a full database of past customers sitting on Gregg's hard drive in an Excel file. Luckily, the file did not contain credit card numbers for the company's customers. Also fortunate was that the thieves had little short-term use for the financial statements from the company that were also on Gregg's hard drive, as stolen financials arouse too much suspicion when sold.

To each of the company's Facebook fans, the thieves e-mailed a similar scam, asking them to update personal data, including credit card numbers, expiration dates, and security codes. Since it appeared to be a legitimate communication directly from the wine company, many of them complied.

Gregg's only consolation was that the thieves did not fire the parting shot that is fairly common on social networking account takeover cases: to cause as much collateral damage to the breached company as possible. In the worst cases, the thieves post a message on the target company's Facebook wall stating that the company is ceasing operation because it failed to adequately protect customer data. In other words, the thieves alert all customers about the data breach for which they are responsible. Occasionally, the wall posting suggests that the customers initiate a class action lawsuit to sue the company for data breach and identity theft. It can be a devastating final blow.

In the wine company's case, because the breached data didn't include customer Social Security numbers, the per-record breach-recovery cost was less than half the average (see Figure 6.1): $91 per record. Still, at 87,436 breached records, the total recovery cost came to $7.9 million. Worse, the company lost most of its customers in the process, and never recovered from that.

(continued)

(*continued*)

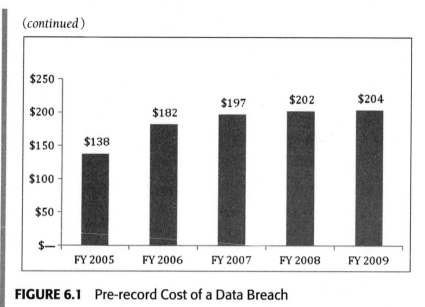

FIGURE 6.1 Pre-record Cost of a Data Breach

Source: "Fifth Annual U.S. Cost of Data Breach Study", Ponemon Institute, 2010.

Secure Mind-Set

Secure technology is at the heart of espionage. Encryption is just sophisticated code-making; hacking is nothing more than modern code-breaking. As we continue to move more of our data online, *securing our digital assets will become the most important form of identity protection.* Spies utilize technology not only to steal information but also to protect it. If secured correctly, maintaining information in a digital format can actually *lower* the risk of data theft because it provides user-level access that is difficult to replicate with physical documents. Whether it is a company laptop, your mobile phone, tape back-ups, wireless networking, or cloud computing (a term used to mean that your data is stored outside of your home or offices on someone else's computer, such as Google's Gmail), technology houses vast quantities of data, making it an ideal target for theft or a sophisticated means of privacy.

The question you should ask yourself is: How can I first protect and then utilize technology to secure identity and intellectual capital?

Secure Your Computer

Digital identity exists in many forms: the data on your hard drive or cell phone; the wireless network at the airport or your hotel; your profile and posts on a social networking site; and the online applications you use, such as like Gmail, Google Docs, and off-site data storage. Spies exploit all of these sources to siphon bits of data (or bytes) and use them to build a complete dossier on your identity, which can then be sold, cloned, or cultivated, all for their financial gain and your loss.

In the simplest form, there are three critical phases to *secure* your digital identity. In this order, take steps to secure:

1. *Your computer* or computing device, such as an iPhone or BlackBerry
2. *The network*, including Ethernet, wireless, and Internet access
3. *Your online presence*, for example, Facebook, e-mail, the cloud, and online applications (covered in depth in Chapter 12, "Defend Online Identity")

Once you have secured your computer, the network, and your online presence, you can begin to use your computer effectively in the fight against data theft.

For many people, a personal computer serves as their primary filing cabinet for financial, legal, and personal records. Your computer can be either an asset or a liability in protecting these records. Unprotected, it is a liability because it is open to:

- *Hackers*, thieves who break in from your Internet or network connection
- *Spyware, malware, and adware*, software that broadcasts your personal information to spies
- *Viruses and worms*, software such as the Bredolab Trojan described in the case study that damages your data—accounting files, spreadsheets, contact lists, word processing docs, tax records, and so on
- *Friendly fraud*, abuse by authorized users—friends, relatives, and acquaintances—who take advantage of your lack of preparation
- *Crimes of opportunity*, committed by people who steal your unprotected information because it's there for the picking

Hire a Professional

I am a strong believer that you get what you pay for. Unless you are a professionally trained computer technician, securing your own computer is a recipe for disaster. You wouldn't fly your own airplane simply because you had been on one before, would you? Or take a wrench to your new electronically controlled car engine just because you used to work on your '72 Gran Torino? Okay, so I didn't even know how to work on my Torino, but you get my point: technology changes too quickly for the average user to keep up with the latest security trends. That is why we hire professionals. But before you do, do your homework:

1. Ask people or businesses you trust who they use to maintain their computers and networks.
2. Use a company that has been around long enough to have a track record for honesty and reliability (five-plus years).
3. Be there—take time out of your day to closely monitor what the technicians are doing to your systems and to verify that everything is aboveboard (your presence in the room greatly decreases the chances that they will defraud you).

I recommend that you make a photocopy of the 15 ways to protect your computer that follow, highlight those items that you need to have completed (many computers already have some of these protections installed on them), and arrange for the technicians to visit you on-site (in your home or office, where you can observe them) to make the necessary upgrades. Don't forget to ask for an estimate of the work to be completed before they start. It won't be exact, but it will give you a general idea. Remember: You may spend tens or hundreds of dollars to protect your computer, but you will be securing thousands of dollars worth of data, and significantly reduce your chances of identity theft in the process.

Fifteen Ways to Protect Your Computer

1. Lock It Up

Physically securing your computer (especially laptops) is the simplest and most overlooked form of computer security available. If criminals don't have physical access to the computer in the first place, theft becomes much more difficult. For further suggestions on protecting mobile data, like laptops, read Chapter 13, "Protect Mobile Data."

2. Deploy Security Software

Many different types of security software have been combined into security suites, such as those provided by Symantec, McAfee, and AVG. Instead of purchasing, installing, updating, and maintaining multiple pieces of software, you can purchase a single suite containing all of the necessary pieces for each computer that you need to protect. Whether you utilize a suite or install programs piece by piece, your security software should be configured to continually update, in order for it to be effective. Security software is generally made up of antivirus, antispyware, firewall, and backup software (discussed, in turn, next).

Visit www.Sileo.com/productreviews for security software recommendations.

3. Install Antivirus and Antispyware

Viruses infect your computer either to destroy data or install spyware. Spyware is any program that launches on your computer without your informed consent and, most often, adversely affects your computer's performance while forwarding your personal information to identity thieves, advertisers, competitors, or anyone with malicious intent (ex-spouses, former employees, etc.).

Spyware comes in many flavors, including *adware* (spying in order to sell you new stuff), *malware* (hijacking your private information), *botnets* (borrowing your computer's processing power to commit crimes), *keystroke loggers* (recording keystrokes you make, including bank login and password information), and others. Spyware is one way that credit card numbers, customer records, buying habits, Social Security numbers, and other pieces of identity are stolen from your system.

Spyware Infection Symptoms

Among the common computer symptoms that you should regard as red flags that your system has been infected by spyware are:

- You begin to receive popup ads.
- Your computer or Internet connection runs slower.
- Your system or network crashes more often.
- The default home page in your browser changes without your consent.
- Your wireless network won't connect.
- Your computer is just "acting strangely."

4. Use a Firewall

A firewall is a device that regulates who or what (from the Internet) has access into your data. It can also be used to regulate what data can leave your computer over the Internet. If you connect to the Internet, and especially if you have high-speed Internet access (DSL, cable modem, T1), it is essential to have a firewall installed and configured. Doing so keeps hackers from getting into your system to steal information.

Many security suites integrate a firewall into their software. In fact, most operating systems, including Windows and OS X also contain integrated firewalls. Software firewalls are generally used for home computing, tend to do a better job at keeping unnecessary information from leaving your computer, and require more processing power (which means they slow your computer down).

Hardware firewalls, by contrast, are commonly used by businesses because they don't sacrifice the performance of individual computers for the sake of security. They can be used to block out specific websites (e.g., if you don't want your employees to visit social networking sites during work, etc.), instant messaging, and file downloads. Your computer technician should be able to make a recommendation based on your specific needs and style.

Points to keep in mind when installing a security suite, firewall, antivirus, or anti-spyware software:

- Make sure you are installing a reputable software package or hardware firewall. For a review of security suites, visit www.Sileo.com/productreviews. Don't settle for a free package. You get what you pay for.
- Ensure that your firewall is configured properly (e.g., turned on by default, set to limit traffic in and data out, protected behind a secure password, and automatically updated with the latest security patches).
- Check that the security software has the latest security updates and is set to auto-update without user intervention.
- Verify that the software is set to periodically run a full system scan (at least weekly).

5. Enable a Pop-up Blocker

Most Internet browsers (Firefox, Safari, Internet Explorer) come standard with a pop-up blocker. If it isn't already, instruct your technician to turn this capability on, as it reduces the chances that you will accidentally download spyware and viruses onto your system.

If you continue to get pop-ups on your computer, *never* give in to temptation to click on any buttons on the screen—including the "NO" or "Decline" buttons, which will also download spyware onto your system. Instead, click on the Windows "X" at the top right corner of your browser to close the window. Pop-ups that show up even though you have a pop-up blocker active are a sure sign that your computer is infected with spyware.

6. Back Up Data

One of the most overlooked forms of security is to make a backup copy of your data. If your computer is damaged in a fire, experiences a hard drive failure, or is corrupted by a virus, malware, or a hacker, the only way to retrieve the data is in the form of a backup copy.

There are many forms of backup, but I recommend those that are contained within a security suite because they make it easy to make regular backups of your data. You can also back up your data to an external drive or flash memory card and store it in a fireproof locked safe. Apple users have an automatic back up utility built in to the computer's operating system, called Time Machine.

7. Configure for Automatic Operating System Updates

Instruct your technician to configure Windows or Mac OS X for automatic security updates, and verify that you have the latest service packs and updates for your operating system and office software. Failing to keep your operating system up to date is like leaving the doors to the castle wide open.

8. Encrypt Your Wireless Connection

Encryption is the process of converting data or information into a cipher (or code) to prevent unauthorized access. It's important to encrypt your wireless network so that your data isn't floating freely on the airwaves, where any hacker can intercept it.

I recommend that you tell your technician to configure your wireless router with WPA2 (not WEP) or an equivalent 802.11i certification. WPA encryption (Wi-Fi Protected Access) is superior to WEP (Wired Equivalency Privacy) because it provides stronger encryption algorithms, and password characters aren't restricted to 0–9 and A–F, as they are on WEP. If, however, you don't have access to WPA, WEP is better than nothing. (Note: It is not necessary to understand the intricacies of these encryption schemes if you have hired a competent security technician who can configure the encryption for you.)

For those of you who are technically minded, WPA2 replaced WPA. Like WPA, WPA2 requires testing and certification by the Wi-Fi Alliance, an industry group. WPA2 implements the mandatory elements of 802.11i (a universal standard of security), but it will not work with some older network cards. In particular, it introduces a new AES-based algorithm, CCMP, which was considered "fully secure" at the time this book was published. Certification began in September 2004; beginning March 13, 2006, to bear the Wi-Fi trademark, WPA2 certification became mandatory for all new devices.[1]

Once your encryption has been enabled, don't broadcast your Service Set Identifier (SSID), a 32-character sequence that uniquely identifies the wireless network, as broadcasting the SSID makes your network visible to neighbors or passersby who might exploit your network for identity theft purposes. Your SSID is what pops up in the "Available Wireless Networks" or "Join Networks" section of your wireless device configuration settings. There is no need to broadcast this to others unless you frequently authorize people to join your wireless network (as would a wireless hotspot like Starbucks). Again, implementing these settings is best left to a professional technician who is comfortable with wireless networks. You'll also want to disable remote administration to prevent hackers from altering your network security settings. Use Media Access Control (MAC) address filtering for access control. Unlike Internet Protocol (IP) addresses, MAC addresses are unique to specific network adapters, so by turning on MAC filtering you can limit network access to just your systems. This ensures that only approved computers can get on your wireless network, which means criminals can't sit outside your office committing Internet crimes (e.g., selling pornography or stolen identities) using your IP address and bandwidth.

9. Encrypt Your Hard Drive

When you encrypt your hard drive using special software, it means that only someone with the key (in this case, a password) can unscramble (decode) the cipher and read the documents. When you encrypt your wireless transmission (see number 8), you scramble the transmission of data until it reaches its destination, where it is unscrambled with the key. That way it cannot be intercepted as it travels through cyberspace.

Although hackers can find ways to break encryption, the process elevates the crime to a whole new level of sophistication, meaning that the average thief will only be able to use the hard drive as a paperweight. In the time it takes to crack the code, the thief could have stolen several more computers that don't contain encrypted hard drives.

Operating systems are beginning to come standard with encryption. You can also purchase stand-alone software that does the job. Either way, you should enlist the help of a seasoned professional to implement the encryption, as there are certain drawbacks and complications (slowing the performance of your system, locking out people who need access, etc.) if done incorrectly.

10. Protect Your Passwords

Now that so much of our financial and even personal lives exist online, protecting our passwords has become more crucial and difficult. It is common for the average Internet user to frequent more than 50 different sites that require login access. That is too many passwords to remember or even keep track of manually, especially if you adhere to the three cardinal rules of password creation:

- Don't use words that can be found in a dictionary, dates or numbers relevant to your life (birthdays, phone numbers), or familiar names (e.g., your pet) as passwords.

- Don't use the same password for multiple accounts.
- Change your passwords frequently.

In the past couple of years, it has also become less safe to simply substitute numbers and characters for related letters. For example, I used to recommend that instead of using a word such as "sunflower" for your password, you spell it with numbers and symbols—for example, *$unfl0w3r*—as this is a pretty easy code to remember, and used to be hard to crack. If, then, you needed to store this information in your address book, contact manager, or wallet, you could simply jog your memory by writing "sun."

Unfortunately, it didn't take thieves long to become wise to this simple method of encryption, and they now regularly substitute @ for a, 1 for L or I, 3 for E, 0 for O, $ for S, and so on when they apply password-cracking software. Thus, this method is no longer as safe as it used to be.

The safest alternative is to create a *random, 13-plus character, alphanumeric symbol, uppercase/lowercase* password that you change frequently. For example:

<Q6VXSd(Qi9Ftv

But who can remember that? No one! Especially if you have more than one password to remember. And we all know that a theory is no good if it is too much trouble to put into practice. Which brings us to a compromise . . .

Password Protection Software

Password protection software stores all of your login information (including passwords) in a secure software vault inside your computer. It is similar to having your web browser automatically save your passwords, but much safer. Web browsers don't typically password-protect your password file, meaning that anyone with access to your computer has access to all of your passwords!

Password protection software stores all your passwords in an encrypted file, which is locked up. The key to unlock it is a single, *master password* that you *do* have to remember. Once this software is installed, in order to log in to any of your online accounts, you must type in your master password.

The benefits of password protection software include:

- *You will use it:* It's easy to create, use, and store a highly secure password for every website that requires login information.

- *Limits user-level access:* Someone who has access to your computer won't automatically also have access to all of your passwords or financial logins.
- *It's easy to update:* Changing passwords frequently is simple and fast.
- *It reduces complexity:* Managing multiple accounts at the same website is a snap (e.g., two Twitter accounts, multiple bank accounts at the same bank).
- *It saves time:* The time you save by maintaining all your passwords in one neat, organized place is fairly significant. Some password protection software will also store other sensitive data, such as credit card numbers, Social Security numbers, investment accounts, and more. This makes it a convenient place to house all of your identity. (See Chapter 10, "Monitor the Signs," for more information about logging and tracking your identity.)

There are, however, some drawbacks to using password protection software. These include:

- *You have all your eggs in one basket:* If someone learns your master password (and has access to your computer), he or she has access to *all* of your logins, not just one. This is the same drawback to using your browser to remember your passwords: it centralizes them all in one place. (In the case of your browser, however, they are centralized and *not* encrypted behind a password.)
- *You run the risk of forgetting your master password:* If you lose or forget your master password, there is *no way* to access your individual logins or passwords. You will have to reestablish them website by website, login by login. Or, if something happens to you and no one else knows your master password, your representatives will have trouble accessing your accounts.
- *It can be inconvenient:* If you travel a great deal and are frequently away from your computer (where your passwords are stored securely) and need to get into password-protected accounts on the web (which you no longer have memorized, if you are using passwords like the example just shown), then password protection software can be frustrating. If this is your situation, you might be better served using the software for the 90 percent of passwords that you don't need while away from your computer and memorizing sophisticated passwords for the 10 percent that you need on a regular basis.

- *You must climb a learning curve:* Setting up login and password information whenever you establish a new online account can occasionally be challenging. Every login scheme is different, so it takes time to become familiar with the program before it is a simple process. Once you have mastered it, however, it becomes an automatic part of registering at a website.

To learn more about password protection software, visit www.Sileo.com/productreviews.

Password protection software isn't for everyone. If you don't use the software, your passwords are probably shorter, more uniform, more common, and somewhat easy for a professional to break. If you do use the software, all of your passwords are centralized in a single location (albeit, behind a computer login password, a password vault password, and at least one layer of encryption, if not more). The important point here is to evaluate the options based on your surfing habits and preferences, balanced against convenience and security.

My final piece of advice on passwords: If you currently use a single password for multiple sites, Windows or Mac logins, or ATM machines, or have passwords made up of birthdates, children's or pets' names, phone numbers, or that don't incorporate both letters and numbers, change them now! Start with your computer and website logins and passwords and then move on to your ATM PIN, debit card, and the rest.

11. Recognize Phishing Scams

Learn to understand and recognize phishing scams. Briefly, a phishing scam is an e-mail disguised to look like it is from a familiar source, such as your financial institution (bank or brokerage), eBay, PayPal, Facebook, Twitter, or a host of other financial and ecommerce companies. The e-mail asks you to log in to the website by clicking on a link within it. This link takes you to another website that looks exactly like that of the legitimate financial institution, where you are asked to input personal information (your identity), which is used by the thief to access your actual account.

To avoid phishing scams, *categorically refuse to enter any information at a website to which you navigated through an e-mail link.* Instead, type the site address into your web browser and go to your account from there. If you have doubts about *any* correspondence you receive through an e-mail, pick up the phone and call the institution that e-mailed you directly. Keep in mind, *no reputable financial or business website* will ask you to click on a link to update your account information. Visit en.wikipedia.org/wiki/Phishing for a more comprehensive explanation of phishing, and to see real-life examples. Phishing schemes evolve so quickly that you need a dynamic way to keep tabs on them, meaning that a book set in print is not the way to do that; a reliable source for a regularly updated definition is.

12. Shop Securely

When shopping online, it's advisable to purchase from a reputable, recognizable company rather than the lowest-priced retailer. Look for these three distinguishing characteristics of secure websites:

- A web address that starts with https:// instead of http://—the "s" stands for secure.
- In the bottom right-hand corner of your browser, look for the small padlock symbol; the closed-lock icon indicates that the site you are buying from uses SSL encryption, a type of computer security that protects your data as it is transmitted. You can double-click on the padlock symbol to see the SSL certificate.
- Increasingly, ecommerce and banking websites are implementing a technology that turns your address bar bright green if the website has obtained an Extended Validation SSL certification (meaning that it is safer than other ecommerce sites). Green is good.

The rule of thumb here is: If the site is not operating on a secure server (i.e., no https and/or no lock), consider shopping elsewhere; otherwise, your credit card will be traveling across the Internet unprotected and you will have no idea who has access to it at the other end. In the absence of these security indicators, either call and make the transaction over the phone or e-mail the company to see if it has a secure website where transactions can take place.

13. Protect Your Laptop

If you have a laptop or notebook computer, you must take extra precautions to protect the data on it. Because of their portability, laptops have a much higher risk of being lost or stolen. When this happens, a thief has as long as he or she needs to crack your passwords. This might mean you should keep sensitive documents out of your notebook entirely, or install disk encryption software that further protects your portable computer. For a full discussion on protecting laptop computers, please refer to Chapter 13, "Protect Mobile Data."

14. Understand the Cloud

"The cloud" is a catch-all term for all the data we store outside of our homes and offices, on other people's servers. Be aware of and try to limit the information you share or store online, including at social networking sites (Facebook, Twitter, LinkedIn, MySpace, YouTube, etc.), in online applications (Google Docs, Hotmail, SalesForce, etc.), at peer-to-peer networking sites (Kazaa, Morpheus, Gnutella, etc.), and on other online tools (blogs, wikis, photo sharing, etc.). Read Chapter 12, "Defend Online Identity," for more about protecting your information in the cloud.

15. Protect Your Spouse/Partner and Children

Don't forget to implement the same safeguards at work and on other computers in your home.

Use Your Computer to Help Prevent Identity Theft

Once your computer is secure, it has many advantages over traditional filing systems:

1. It is locked anytime you are not using the computer (thanks to passwords and encryption).
2. You can allow different levels of access for different people (thanks to user profiles that are based on usernames and passwords). With a filing cabinet, one key lets everyone into everything.
3. You can store vast quantities of data without taking up physical space. This eliminates the need to destroy physical documents, which saves you time.

4. By using your computer, you can shut down one of the most vulnerable avenues of identity theft—mail. By receiving statements and paying bills online, you are less vulnerable to red-flagging (mail theft).

5. When data arrives via e-mail, Internet, and other digital sources, it is already partially filed, as it already exists on your hard drive. You may choose to save it in a different location, but either way, it is protected. It never exists in an unlocked state, like mail does.

6. You can review online statements more quickly, enabling you to catch inconsistencies faster than if you were notified by law enforcement or a creditor. Identity theft victims who monitored their accounts online discovered the fraud, on average, in eight days and incurred an average loss of $3,927. In contrast, victims who were contacted by a debt collector or creditor had an average of $8,522 stolen and it took them an average of 156 days to detect the fraud.[2] Rapid detection is half the battle!

7. You can add additional layers of protection quite easily if your data is extremely valuable. For less than $100, you can buy software that encrypts your hard drive (turns your data into a collection of nonsense to anyone who doesn't have the encryption key or password).

Here's my recommendation: *Replace paper statements* that arrive through the mail, and that may subsequently be left exposed on desks for long periods of time, with online statements that are automatically stored in your computer. By replacing paper bills, statements, and checks with electronic versions (on the Internet), you eliminate the risk of their being stolen out of your mailbox or off your desk (discussed in the tasks section of Chapter 4, "Eliminate the Source"). The next time you receive a statement of any kind in the mail, call the customer service number on the statement, or log on to the company's website and configure your account for electronic statements. Follow up, to make sure that your paper statements are stopped. Over the course of a month, you should have switched most of your account statements from paper to electronic versions. Don't forget to opt out of information sharing while you are on the phone with the companies.

I also strongly urge you to stop paying bills through the mail with paper checks. As you have probably noticed, I emphasize throughout the book that one of the best ways to prevent identity theft is to stop using the mail system to transmit sensitive documents.

Using Electronic Statements

Most electronic statements come in the form of an Adobe Acrobat (or PDF) file. These can be saved directly to your hard drive in a folder named for their specific purpose (e.g., 2009 Bank Statements—Account 4299).

When you are online viewing your first statement, set up auto-alerts (if the company offers them) that warn you about any major activity on the account. For example, most financial institutions let you set up auto-alerts, sent to you via e-mail when certain transactions occur on your account. This is a very effective way to monitor your finances on a daily basis without much time investment (see Chapter 10, "Monitor the Signs").

There are several ways you can pay your bills that do not involve sending a check through the mail.

- *Auto-Pay:* Set up auto-pay by credit card. You can generally do this with most major companies (phone bill, utilities, cable TV, insurance, etc.). You can also pay by credit card on a month-by-month basis on most websites. This isn't as convenient, but it gives you more control over your charges. I prefer this option, as it gives you an easy method to dispute charges, should you need to do so (you call the credit card company and freeze the payment until your dispute is settled). In addition, your liability is only $50 if you report fraud in a reasonable time frame, which is usually established by each individual company.
- *Electronic Funds Transfer:* Since you cannot pay a credit card with a credit card (well, technically you can, but we won't go into that), you will have to pay by other means. You can set up an electronic funds transfer between your bank and the bank of the company to which you owe money. For example, many insurance agencies don't allow credit card payments, but they will automatically deduct your premium each month directly from your bank account. I use this option when the credit card option is not available, but *only after* I have established a trusting relationship with the company that will be withdrawing the funds.

- *Bill Pay:* You can use an electronic bill payment service, which is offered by most banks, brokerages, and many other businesses. This is a good third option. Most of the electronic bill payment services still cut paper checks and send them through the mail. While this reduces the risk that an outgoing check will be stolen from your mailbox, it does not lower the risk of it being stolen from the bill payer's mail, or in transit. The good news is, the account number that generally appears on bill-pay checks is the bank's, not yours.

Action Item Checklist: Secure the Systems

Hire a professional to secure your computer.
Physically store your computer in a safe and secure place.
Implement a security software suite.
Use antivirus and antispyware software.
Back up your data regularly.
Enable a pop-up blocker.
Install a firewall.
Configure your computer to automatically update all protection and antivirus software, pop-up blockers, and firewalls.
Encrypt your wireless connection.
Encrypt your hard drive.
Create random 13-plus character passwords, and protect them.
Look into password protection software.
Be aware of and learn to recognize phishing scams.
Shop securely online from reputable, recognizable companies.
Password-protect your computer, and lock it when you are not using it.
Replace paper statements that arrive through the mail with online and electronic versions.
Stop paying bills through the mail with paper checks. Instead use auto-pay, electronic funds transfer, or online bill pay.
Implement all safeguards for your spouse or partner and family members.

Business Relevance

Technology is the focal point of data breach and workplace identity theft because corporations create, transmit, and store so many pieces of information digitally that it becomes a highly attractive target. This book is not intended to address the complex maze that larger organizations face in protecting their technological and digital assets. Rather, the purpose of this book is to begin to familiarize business employees, executives, and vendors with the various security issues facing them.

The task, then, is to develop a capable team (internal and external) to address these issues. In my experience, the following technology-related issues pose the greatest data-loss threats inside organizations:

- *Laptop Theft:* According to the Ponemon Institute, 36 percent[3] of reported breaches are due to a lost or stolen laptop.
- *Mobile Data Theft:* Thumb drives, CDs, DVDs, tape backups, smart phones
- *Malware:* Software that infects corporate systems, allowing criminals inside these networks
- *Hacking:* Breaking into your computer system from the outside, using networks, wireless connections, remote access, and your Internet pipeline
- *Wireless Theft:* Wireless connections to the Internet in airports, hotels, cafés, and conferences
- *Insider Theft:* When someone in the IT department (or elsewhere) decides to make extra money by selling your data

According to the Ponemon Institute, "Thirty-six percent of all cases in this year's study involved lost or stolen laptop computers or other mobile data-bearing devices. Data breaches concerning lost, missing, or stolen laptop computers are more expensive than other incidents. Specifically, in this year's study, the per-victim cost for a data breach involving a lost or stolen laptop was just under $225, over $30 more than if a laptop or mobile device was not involved." See Figure 6.2.

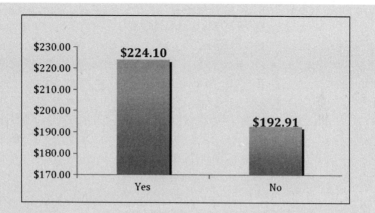

FIGURE 6.2   Lost or Stolen Device

Source: "Fifth Annual U.S. Cost of Data Breach Study," Ponemon Institute, 2010.

In conjunction with the steps discussed earlier in this chapter, here are some additional guidelines your business can follow to better protect sensitive information:

1. Encrypt sensitive customer information.
2. Educate your customers on using sophisticated passwords (as explained previously).
3. Create personalized identification numbers that are not based on customer identity (SSN, account numbers, etc.).
4. Use truncated account numbers or other identifying information in customer e-mails to let them know the e-mail could only be coming from you.
5. Adhere to the Payment Card Industry (PCI) Security Standards Council and any legislation regulating how your industry controls data.
6. Eliminate embedded links in all e-mails to your customers so they know that any links they do receive under your company's name are probably phishing attempts. Educate them about your link policy.
7. Enlist your customers to quickly detect fraud (see Chapter 10, "Monitor the Signs").
8. Prepare and implement a data breach response plan.

To learn more about products that can help you protect your company's digital information, please visit www.Sileo.com/productreviews.

7

The Fourth Mind-Set: Lock the Docs

Technology is a significant source of identity theft and data breach. That said, according to research, your risk of physical document theft is still considerably higher than electronic theft. For one reason, as we all turn our attention more toward protecting ourselves technologically, thieves are taking advantage of good old-fashioned document theft.

Victim #1,477,377: The Inside Job

Carmen's family was robbed when she was 11. She will never forget how sick it made her feel that someone had been in her home, prowling around. That is why Carmen, now 36 and with a house larger than most people dream of owning, takes particular pride in, and spent a fortune on, home security. She grew up "thinking like a thief," and takes great precautions to protect her home from the outside in.

She lives in a gated community with a security service that monitors residents' homes 24 hours a day. She has installed a $20,000 motion-sensitive burglar alarm and video surveillance system, and owns two German shepherds. On all of her doors are double-deadbolts, which are connected to a thumbprint scanner. When someone wants to enter the house, they must press their thumbs against a pad just outside any of the doorways. Four people have access by thumbprint to Carmen's house: her mother, sister, cleaning lady, and best friend.

Carmen describes her home as a "safe house." She shreds every piece of paper that leaves the house; uses encryption technology on her computer, Internet connection, and wireless network; and only mails documents directly from the post office. Her wallet contains one credit card, her driver's license, and a picture of her nephew; she does not carry checks. The documents in her car are locked up.

In spite of all her precautions, Carmen's identity was stolen completely, without her knowledge. She found out two years after it happened, when her identity was given to the police during an arrest for a crime that she had nothing to do with. The perpetrator (who was not the original identity thief, but someone who had purchased a "new" identity on the Internet) held up a pharmacy at gunpoint and was caught because of a flat tire.

What was the weakness in Carmen's security setup? The way she stored private documents—or rather, the way she didn't store them. She had left tax documents on her desk for weeks before filing them securely.

Who was the thief? It turned out to be a painter who had asked to use the upstairs bathroom because the downstairs bathroom was wet with paint. The police believe that the painter used the small photocopier in Carmen's home office to make copies of several of her documents. And because none of her papers were ever identified as missing, she never suspected foul play. The painter was later caught stealing documents from another job site and confessed to the police to stealing Carmen's information, as well.

Lock up your vital documents as if they were cold, hard cash, because to an identity thief, they are. *Lock your docs!*

Lock Mind-Set

Spies operate from a mind-set of secrecy and behind a perimeter of locks and classification systems. As we learned in the last two chapters, they keep only what they need and destroy any information that has no further use. But their secrecy goes even further. They operate out of "safe houses," which are information-tight despite often being in the middle of enemy territory. In the world of espionage, nothing is more valuable, or damaging, than a top-secret document. And nothing is more effective at keeping the enemy from accessing it than to *physically lock it up.*

Systematically classify and lock up all private documents that could lead to identity theft if they were to fall into the wrong hands. Ask yourself in regard to *each* identity document: How would you classify the damage done if this specific document were stolen and sold? Lock accordingly.

> A quick note on the title of this chapter, "Lock the Docs": Locking techniques take two basic forms, physical and digital. This chapter focuses on the *physical* types of locks, including safes, locking filing cabinets, and even office doors, whereas the previous chapter, "Secure the Systems," described how to lock *digital* data using passwords, encryption, firewalls, security software, and other tools. The two forms of locking often work in conjunction with one another, as when you physically lock your computer. Don't apply either locking technique in isolation from the other mind-sets.

Create a Safe House

A safe house is not just a physical location; it is also a way of thinking. Creating a safe house should prompt you to think about who has access into the house (and, thus, your information) and what data leaves the house (access in/data out). Let me explain.

Think of a safe house as a centralized repository of every piece of intelligence that a spy has collected or is protecting. It contains dossiers (vital documents) on the spy's targets and informants, information about his or her true identity and aliases, and links to his or her employer and maybe even other spies who are a part of the network. Because of the value of this information, there are controls on who has access into the house (access in) and on what data is allowed out of the house (data out). Creating a safe house by controlling access in and data out is a mind-set of its own.

These are the same controls that you must implement in your home and office. Simply put, anytime a piece of data goes out of the house (via trash, telephone, mail, e-mail, wireless network, human carrier, etc.) or someone is allowed (or illegally gains access) into the house (friends, family, guests, contract laborers, domestic help, thieves), you should have safeguards in place to protect your essential identity documents. Remember, the better acquainted you are with the thief, the greater the damage he or she can do to your identity.

> *Those victims who knew their perpetrator personally were less likely to be notified of the breach, suffered from the more damaging debit fraud, and spent more than twice as many hours (53 hours versus 22 hours) resolving their frauds.*
>
> —*"2009 Identity Fraud Survey Report,"*
> *Javelin Strategy & Research*

In recent years, burglars have increasingly broken into homes in order to steal documents, rather than electronics and jewelry. When you centralize all of your documents in a single place (office filing cabinet or fire safe), it makes it that much easier for them to steal it. As a result, it is now imperative that we physically secure our document storage so that it cannot be easily picked up and carried away. This may mean having your fire safe bolted into the foundation of your home, utilizing a safe that is too heavy to move quickly and easily, or creating a *safe room* of your own.

Safe Room

You may find it easier to designate an entire room or space in your home (or in your office) to store sensitive documents. Here is one example of how to creatively protect your documents. Designate a small closet as your safe room. If you have a closet in your office, this is a convenient place to start. If you would like greater security (and don't mind sacrificing a bit of convenience), use a closet in your basement. After you have chosen your safe room, I recommend taking the following precautions:

- Have a solid-core door installed on the closet, to increase the security.
- On the door, install a keypad lock that allows you and your family easy access inside without having to use a key.
- Inside the closet, install your fire-resistant filing cabinets (or regular filing cabinets if you are not concerned about protecting your documents against fire).
- File all of your identity documents (examples in the next section) in these cabinets, and keep the door locked at all times, especially when

you leave the office or house. Remove documents *only* when you need to work on them, and return them promptly when you are done.

I realize that creating a safe room may seem to you like overkill. I thought the same thing—until my parents were robbed. In their case, the criminals stole a filing cabinet drawer full of documents, because the filing cabinet itself was connected to a desk and was too bulky to take in its entirety. Had the office door or even the filing cabinet been locked, the thieves would not have had time to break the locks and steal the docs.

Essential Identity Documents and How to Lock Them

Table 7.1 lists some of your essential (vital) identity documents, where you should store them, and where to store duplicate copies. For all documents, consult with your lawyer, accountant, or tax advisor regarding how long you need to store them, as times can vary.

Table 7.1   Essential Identity Docs and Where to Store

Type of Storage	Document(s)	Keep a Copy?	Where to Store Duplicates
Bank safe deposit box	Birth certificates; death certificates; marriage license; adoption, citizenship, divorce papers	Yes	Secured fire safe or safe room
	Inventory and photos of household property	Yes	Secured fire safe or safe room
	Property deeds, titles, bills of sale, car title, mortgage documents	Yes	Secured fire safe or safe room
	List of location of important papers	Yes	Secured fire safe or safe room, a secure off-site location (friend or relative's fire safe, attorney's office, etc.)
	Insurance policies	Yes	Secured fire safe or safe room

The documents listed in Table 7.2 are those you need to protect against fire, flood, and theft.

Table 7.2 Docs to Protect Against Fire, Flood, and Theft

Type of Storage	Document(s)	Keep a Copy?	Where to Store Duplicates
Secured fire safe or fire-rated locking filing cabinet	Tax returns; supporting documents for past seven years; Social Security cards	No	—
	Passports	Yes	Secured fire safe or safe room; also, secure a copy of your passport in a different location from the original when you travel
	Bank account information	Yes	Secure off-site location
	List of passwords, PINs, and account numbers	No	It is too difficult to keep an updated version off-site unless you use an electronic solution (online document vault).
	List of all assets, including brokerage and mutual fund accounts, stocks, bonds, bank accounts, real estate and employee-benefit accounts	Yes	Secure off-site location
	Backup copies of computer documents (CDs, DVDs, tape backups, disks)	Yes	Secure off-site location
	Lease agreements; loan documents; rental agreements; vehicle purchase agreements	No	—

Table 7.3   Docs to Protect Against Theft

Type of Storage	Document(s)	Keep a Copy?	Where to Store Duplicates
Locking filing cabinet or secured computer	Bank statements	No	—
	Cancelled checks	No	—
	Investments, securities, mutual fund statements	No	—
	Credit card statements	No	—
	Monthly mortgage statements	No	—
	Phone, utilities, cable, cellular statements	No	—
Wallet	Driver's license or other photo ID	Yes	Secured fire safe or safe room
	Auto insurance card	Yes	Secured in car
	Emergency contacts	Yes	Secured fire safe or safe room
	Blood type, list of allergies, medications	Yes	Secured fire safe or safe room
	Credit cards and other cards	Yes	Secured fire safe or safe room

The documents specified in Table 7.3 are those you need to safeguard against theft.

Lock Your Vital Physical Documents

Buy a fire safe or fire-rated filing cabinet for your home. This is where you will store your essential identity documents. Go to your local office supply store, or visit www.Sileo.com/productreviews for our reviews on the best fire safes and fire-rated filing cabinets. Save money by purchasing a filing cabinet that is also fire-rated, eliminating the need for both a fire safe and a locking filing cabinet.

Your safe or cabinet should meet these minimum requirements:

- Capable of withstanding 1500°F for 30 minutes
- Lockable by key or combination
- Heavy enough to discourage theft, or capable of securing to the ground
- Preferably waterproof (in case of fire, your house will get wet)
- Ideally, buy stackable units so that your safe storage can expand along with your document requirements

Lock your essential identity documents according to Tables 7.1 to 7.3. Take the following steps:

1. Collect all of the documents that you need to put in a bank safe deposit box (banks charge about $50 per year for a document-sized drawer).
2. Photocopy each of these documents and place the copy in your fire safe or fire-rated cabinet. For easy reference, keep a log of every document that is stored in your bank deposit box (especially for your spouse or partner, who might not be as familiar with the contents).
3. Put the documents in the bank's safety deposit box and put one key in your fire safe and another in a completely different location (e.g., in a secure place at your office). Make sure that your spouse or partner also can get into the safety deposit box, as banks generally seal these boxes upon death of the owner if there are no surviving cosigners. These documents are the most important ones in your life and should be kept indefinitely.
4. Collect and file the remainder of the documents that belong in a fire safe. Set up one hanging file folder per year, with documents separated into manila folders by subject (bank, brokerage, home, etc.). I suggest keeping seven years of records, because that is an easy number to remember and is an ample amount of time to store most documents. I use a slightly larger fire-rated filing cabinet, to avoid having to purchase both a fire safe and a locking filing cabinet.
5. Collect and file the remainder of the documents in a locking filing cabinet. Each time you file the latest version of these documents, shred any statements that have outlived their life span. Within months you will have a filing cabinet that is simplified and up to date.

6. Clean up your desk, files, and mail area. Use safety as the mandatory impetus for removing sensitive papers from your desk, drawers, and elsewhere; centralize them in one secure location.

7. If you own a business, use only locking trash dumpsters, and give the trash company a key to the padlock. Locking up your trash can greatly decrease your legal liability. As of June 1, 2005, businesses are required to destroy all consumer information before discarding it in the trash. And as stated in Chapter 5, the Fair & Accurate Credit Transaction Act (FACTA) Disposal Rule states that "any person who maintains or otherwise possesses consumer information for a business purpose" must properly destroy the information prior to disposal. FACTA further states that every person and/or business must take "reasonable measures" to protect against unauthorized access to the use of the information in connection with its disposal.[1]

Securing Your Mail

In the modern world of espionage, a majority of communication between a spy and his or her network takes place via computer. Sending documents electronically is very low-profile, easy-to-protect (encrypt), and immediate, giving counterspies (thieves) little time to intercept the data. Still, there are times when information cannot be sent electronically. In such circumstances, spies use a "dead drop," a secret location where materials can be left by one person and retrieved by another.

> The information in this section is doubly important for those readers who do not have or choose not to use a computer to receive online statements and pay bills.
>
> As discussed earlier in the book, it is important to take preventive steps that fit with your lifestyle. If you choose not to receive statements or correspondence on your computer, the chances are good that you won't implement the changes I recommend for securing your identity electronically. Instead, you should implement the noncomputing version of protecting your mail, described in this section.

Many people still do not believe that mail can be stolen so easily. They think of mail delivery as another public service that rarely falters (like the electricity to your home, for example). Because it is so convenient to mail documents, we continue to drop them in the box, ignoring the very real risk of doing so.

Think for a minute about the risk of mailing sensitive documents incorrectly:

- At a recent lecture sponsored by the U.S. Postal Inspection Service (the mail police), the inspector responsible for my region of the country strongly recommended that people *not* leave incoming or outgoing mail in unlocked mailboxes, like the ones in front of their homes.
- He also recommended that we not put outgoing mail in the blue USPS drop boxes, even those in front of post offices. He said that these boxes are regularly broken into, or are too often "dummy boxes" that don't even belong to the mail service, or have had the bottoms cut out and replaced by cardboard so that the contents can be picked up after dark by "midnight mailmen" (identity thieves). Many of these crimes are committed by members of methamphetamine drug rings that steal identities to fund their illegal drug activities.

Lock Your Mail Against Theft

The best solution is simple: *Stop using the mail to send and receive identity documents* (as just described). Unfortunately, it's not always possible to implement. Therefore, I suggest these alternatives:

- *Install a lock box.* Install a locking mailbox that only you can access. These generally have a mail slot that allows the postal service to put mail into them. Many newer neighborhoods already have some form of locking mailboxes.
- *Rent a P.O. box.* If a locking mailbox is not possible for you, rent a P.O. box at your local post office and have sensitive documents sent there. It is a little less convenient, but assures you much more privacy.
- *Mail in person.* When mailing sensitive documents, walk them into the post office and hand them to a postal worker. If it is after hours, drop the mail through an internal slot in the building. If there is no internal

mailing slot, wait and mail it the next day. This eliminates the most vulnerable stages of mailing.

- *Use overnight delivery services.* Have identity documents sent by UPS or FedEx, and make sure to require a signature for delivery. Taking this precaution makes the information harder to steal, and you can track package location at any time, which will alert you if the document isn't delivered in a timely manner or has been diverted elsewhere.
- *Send checks to the bank.* Have sensitive documents (like new checks or credit cards) sent to your bank rather than to your home address. Pick them up there.
- *Watch for cards.* When you are expecting new credit cards through the mail, keep an eye out for them and call the credit card company if they don't arrive in 7 to 10 days.
- *Retrieve mail quickly.* If you are unable to install a locking mailbox and don't have access to P.O. boxes, retrieve any mail you receive within an hour or two of delivery. This lowers the theft-exposure time of your mail.

Finally, review Chapter 4, "Eliminate the Source," for tips on cutting down the amount of mail that is delivered to your home.

Twenty-five percent of consumers have stopped using paper statements or bills. Avoiding the use of paper bills and banking statements altogether is a surefire way to eliminate paper-based identity theft.

—*"2009 Identity Fraud Survey Report,"*
Javelin Strategy & Research

Action Item Checklist: Lock the Docs

- ☐ Create a safe house or a safe room.
- ☐ Purchase a fire safe or fire-rated filing cabinet and secure it to the foundation of your home or office (if feasible).
- ☐ Lock your essential documents according to Tables 7.1 to 7.3.
- ☐ Lock your mail (and mailbox) against theft:

- Use a locking mailbox or rent a P.O. box.
- Mail sensitive documents in person.
- Have identity documents sent by UPS or FedEx (with tracking).
- Have new checks sent to your bank for pickup.
- Retrieve mail within an hour or two of delivery, and watch for new credit cards.

Business Relevance

Locking up sensitive documents is one of the most important and underutilized ways to protect company data. Of the individuals surveyed by the Ponemon Institute, 56 percent state that over 50 percent of their company's sensitive or confidential information is contained within paper documents.[2] Since 49 percent of all breaches involved paper, locking up what cannot be eliminated or destroyed is essential. To get you firmly into the business mind-set of thinking like a spy, start with this simple three-step classification process:

1. *Classification:* Set up a classification scheme. For example, you might have four levels of access: public, internal, classified, and top secret.
   - *Public* documents are the only documents meant to be seen by outsiders (the public). This might include sales and marketing materials, websites, public filings, and the like.
   - *Internal* documents are those appropriate for employees of the company to see, but inappropriate for outsiders. These are generally not high-risk documents, still it's better to keep them confidential, just in case.
   - *Classified* documents are a security risk if the wrong people see them, either internally or externally. Only certain employees and executives would have access to these documents (see step 2). Classified documents might include human resource files,

(continued)

(continued)

customer lists, product development papers, department financials, strategy frameworks, and so on.

- *Top secret* documents are those meant for only a small number of very carefully vetted people at the company. Top secret documents tend to include trade secrets (e.g., the recipe for Coke), intellectual capital, merger and acquisition data, and proprietary financials.

2. *User-level Access:* Set up a system of locking that grants only qualified individuals access to the corresponding level of confidentiality. Top secret documents would be stored in a safe accessible by, and known to, a limited number of people. Confidential documents might be stored in locking filing cabinets or in a safe room that is managed or monitored by a gatekeeper. Internal documents would probably be stored in filing cabinets (preferably, locking) and not be easily accessible to others, especially after hours (by cleaning staff, visitors). Public documents need not be locked.

3. *Education and Accountability:* You must educate your employees and executives on the classification framework you develop, or it will go unused. Because this type of classification and user-level access relies on the honesty of the participants (e.g., anyone can pick up and read a top secret file if it is left out in the open), there has to be fairly serious consequences if protocol is breached. Communicate a clear picture of what action(s) will be taken against the offending party when one of the following happens:

- You discover someone accessing documents above his or her access level.
- You encounter documents that are unclassified or improperly classified.
- You find locking filing cabinets unlocked, safe rooms unmonitored, or classified documents out in the open.

8

The Fifth Mind-Set: Evaluate the Risk

In espionage, making rational, immediate decisions is paramount. A great deal of preparation goes into making wise decisions with regard to sensitive information. This chapter is the first of two aimed at giving you the tools to detect acts of fraud, social engineering, and identity theft in the earliest stages.

Victim #6,777,763: Social Engineering at the Gym

One day at the gym, a woman watched over Michelle's shoulder while she dialed the combination to her locker. Having observed her habits for several weeks, the woman knew that Michelle drove a nice car and that she exercised three times a week after work for approximately an hour. The following week, just after Michelle left the locker room to work out, the woman broke into Michelle's locker and stole her wallet. And while she was at it, the thief took an extra second to make a note of Michelle's cell phone number. That's how identity thieves work: They collect small, imperceptible pieces of data until they add up to a complete, valuable identity.

When Michelle returned from working out, she discovered that her wallet was gone. She walked to her car to make sure she hadn't left it there, and as she was unlocking the car, received a call on her cell phone. The caller identified herself as an agent from her bank, saying that they had caught someone trying to use her debit card to cash out her account. The agent explained that

(continued)

(*continued*)

the security guard at the bank had stopped the thief, taken her into custody, and needed Michelle to positively identify the contents of her wallet.

For security purposes, the bank agent asked Michelle to verify her account information, including Social Security number and mother's maiden name. The agent then suggested that Michelle immediately change her PIN number while they were on the phone together before any further damage could be done. In a panic, Michelle gave the agent the information, including her current PIN number. After all, the agent knew her name, her bank account, and her cell phone number, so the request seemed entirely plausible.

The bank agent turned out to be another member of an identity theft ring, and had just "socially engineered" (conned) Michelle into giving away even more damaging information by establishing a relationship of trust using the pieces of identity the first thief had collected from her locker.

By systematically collecting Michelle's identity, the identity theft ring drained her bank account, charged thousands of dollars to her credit cards, set up "official" driver's licenses with her information (and other people's pictures), used the licenses to steal six rental cars in six different states, and purchased plane tickets to fly across the country under Michelle's name.

Within months, warrants for Michelle's arrest had been issued in several states, and she subsequently spent more than two years battling multiple identities under her name across the country. Worse, because there was no federal jurisdiction over the crime of identity theft (and at the time of this writing, there still is no federal jurisdiction), Michelle had to fight the battle mostly alone (with the help of her lawyer), one local jurisdiction at a time.

Everything Michelle suffered could have been avoided if she had had a keener sense of observation and evaluation.

Evaluate Mind-Set

Spies are aware of virtually everything happening around them. They are able to make quick decisions because they are prepared at all times to confront the enemy. Their skills of observation and evaluation prepare them to preempt fraud and social engineering (defined as the act of obtaining confidential information by manipulation) *before* they expose valuable intelligence.

By learning to evaluate offers to share data before we act, we can arm our-selves against all these types of social engineering:

- Identity theft: phishing, pharming, shoulder surfing
- Financial fraud: investment and get-rich-quick schemes
- Corporate espionage: the inside job, double agents, and the like

Evaluation is a process of applying common sense and natural instinct to the constant barrage of information requests we receive. It helps us determine whom we can trust and, more importantly, *how we can trust*. And it protects the most commonly exploited source of data leakage of all: the *human source*.

The process of evaluation begins by asking questions:

- Why should I share this information?
- How do I know these parties are trustworthy?
- How will they use my data? What are my options?

The fifth and sixth mind-sets, *evaluate the risk* and *interrogate the enemy* are actually two parts of the same process, which, when combined, give you the tools to stop social engineering and fraud in your home and your workplace. We observe a situation, pause to make a judgment on what is happening, and then act on what we conclude. For example, we see someone lurking in the sha-dows of a doorway in the next block (*observe*), make the decision to cross the street, away from potential danger (*evaluate*), and then cross the street (*act*).

Spies are masters at this process. When they are out in the field spying, they are hyperaware of their surroundings. Their skills of observation and evaluation include:

- Monitoring any changes in their environment (which can signal trouble)
- Ignoring their assumptions about a situation (things aren't always as they appear)
- Watching their backs in the field (you never know who the enemy is)
- Maintaining a healthy skepticism about sharing information
- Making snap judgments about issues of risk and safety

We must learn to use these same skills to protect our identity. But we are at a distinct disadvantage, because we are distracted.

Social Engineers Exploit
Our Distracted Minds

Let's be honest, many of us are walking around in a fog of distraction. We talk on our cell phones between bites of a bagel as we steer the car to our next destination, and have the nerve to ask our kids to pipe down so that we can think. Yeah, right. To the outside observer, anyone who actually stops and watches us, we must look like zombies.

To those of you who are not more or less constantly distracted, I congratulate and envy you. James Woods, the actor, is one of those; he has acute powers of observation, as the following story illustrates.

Just weeks before the tragic 9/11 attacks, James Woods flew cross-country to Los Angeles. On the flight, he noticed four well-dressed Middle Eastern men traveling together. In an interview with Seymour Hersh of the *New Yorker*, in June of 2002, Woods commented "I watch people like a moviemaker. . . . I thought these guys were either terrorists or FBI guys."

Woods, viewing the situation through the lens of a moviemaker, observed what many of us wouldn't have:

"These guys were in synch—dressed alike. They didn't have a drink and were not talking to the stewardess. None of them had a carry-on or a newspaper. Nothing."

Woods was suspicious that the four men were "casing" the plane, so he alerted the flight attendant. According to Hersh's article, when Woods was later shown photographs of the 9/11 hijackers, he thought he recognized two of them—Hamza Alghamdi, who flew on United Flight 175, which destroyed the south tower of the World Trade Center, and Khalid Almihdhar, who was on American Airlines Flight 77, which struck the Pentagon.

Woods told Hersh that he recognized one of the men because of his "pointy hair," and the other because he resembled one of the characters in the movie version of spy novelist John le Carre's *The Little Drummer Girl*. James Woods's heightened sense of observation and evaluation triggered his instinct of danger. He had noticed other passengers acting out of character (no luggage or reading materials, dressed identically, and isolated from the flight attendants), and took action. If his hunch had been taken seriously, the outcome of 9/11 might have been very different.

The American poet Theodore Roethke said, "A mind too active is no mind at all." Identity thieves take advantage of our distracted minds. We must slow down and learn to observe our surroundings and evaluate what we see, especially when our identity is "in play."

Some people are naturally more observant. They notice when the tire on their car is low without consciously thinking about it. They look to see if someone is behind them at the ATM machine as a matter of habit. The rest of us need help developing and using our powers of observation. Because we are in a hurry or have other things on our mind, we act without thinking things through much of the time.

Observation is a difficult and intangible skill to teach (and learn), because it is really nothing more than seeing what is already in front of us. For example, look at the diagram in Figure 8.1 and quickly count the number of squares.

Before I reveal the answer, let me ask you: Were you able to come up with your number in five seconds or less? I have found when speaking to audiences that people tend to be more concerned with the speed of arriving at an answer than with its accuracy. Here, though, I preconditioned you to answer rapidly by the way that I gave the instructions.

If your answer was fewer than 17 squares, take more time with the puzzle— but after reading through the following heightened observation process:

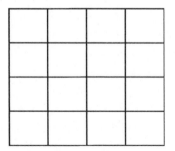

FIGURE 8.1 How Many Squares Do You See?

The author just suggested that many people are distracted. Could that be me? He is attempting to teach me about the powers of observation and is giving me a test to see if my answer is preconditioned.

Don't answer immediately; there is something that I am probably missing here. What haven't I thought of? Could there be a different number of squares than the obvious answer?

Get out now. Not just outside, but beyond the trap of the programmed electronic age so gently closing around so many people at the end of our century. Go outside, move deliberately, then relax, slow down, look around. Do not jog. Do not run. Forget about blood pressure and arthritis, cardiovascular rejuvenation and weight reduction. Instead, pay attention to everything that abuts the rural road, the city street, the suburban boulevard. Walk. Stroll. Saunter. Ride a bike, and coast along a lot. Explore.

—*John Stilgoe, Outside Lies Magic*

The squares can be counted in groups of 1 (for a total of 16 squares), as well as be combined into squares made up of 4 smaller squares (9 combinations), 9 smaller squares (4 combinations), and 16 smaller squares (1 combination). The correct answer is 30. If you didn't get it right, don't feel bad; it took me five tries and several sheets of paper. My powers of observation used to reach about as far as my eyelashes. If you counted all 30 on the first try, perhaps you should look into espionage as a full-time profession.

The point of this exercise has little to do with arriving at the correct answer. It is to demonstrate that our assumptions, biases, and natural preconditioning are very powerful, and can get in the way of effective observation. In this example, we were preconditioned to find the answer to the puzzle quickly rather than to think about it. Is it because we believe that the faster we answer, the smarter we appear? Is it our competitive nature? A desire to impress others?

Regardless of the source of preconditioning, pointing it out tends to eliminate the conditioning. If I were to give you a second puzzle, you would examine it more closely, I assure you. Voíla! Your powers of observation have already been sharpened.

To increase our powers of observation in regard to our identity, we must first know what to look for, what preconditions exist, and how to respond to them.

The Privacy Reflex:
Trigger, Reflex, and Response

When I am training corporate executives, managers, and employees how to detect fraud and social engineering (manipulative information-gathering techniques), I take them through what it feels like to be conned. In other words, I actually socially engineer them several times throughout the presentation so that they begin to sense reflexively when more fraud is coming. There is no substitute for experiencing this firsthand.

> Experience social engineering for yourself by taking three minutes to watch the social engineering video at www.Sileo.com/social-engineering. I urge you to do so, as this will better prepare you to apply the *trigger*, *reflex*, and *response* techniques discussed in this section.

The Trigger: Requests for Identity

Spies are trained to react instantly when anyone asks for information of any kind, whether it is theirs or someone else's. The trigger, or what causes you to be on high alert, is actually very simple: It is the appearance of your identity in any form (wallet, credit card, tax form, passport, driver's license, etc.). Anytime someone requests or has access to any of the names, numbers, or attributes that make up your identity, or to the paper, plastic, digital, or human data where your identity lives, the trigger should trip, sounding an alarm in your head.

Here are some examples of triggers:

- When you are pulling out your wallet, purse, checkbook, or credit card
- When you are putting a document into the trash or filing cabinet
- When someone is requesting information about you on Facebook, LinkedIn, and other such sites
- When someone requests information about your company, logins, or coworkers
- When you are sending a piece of mail
- When you are clicking on a link in an e-mail

- When you are entering data into a website
- When you are using an ATM machine or PIN pad
- When you receive a call requesting information
- When you notice sensitive documents lying on your desk at home or work
- When you are opening an account
- When anyone requests your personal information
- When you are voluntarily sharing any piece of your identity
- When you are involved in any sort of money or credit transaction
- When you are answering a survey or entering a contest
- Anytime you fill out forms that request a piece of your identity

When your identity is being requested in *any way*, slow down and ask yourself: *Is the risk of giving this piece of identity away in this specific situation worth the benefit?*

The Reflex: Hogwash!

By training, when a spy's trigger has been, well, triggered, a specific word, phrase, or picture automatically pops into his or her head, whether he or she thinks consciously about it or not.

If the word (also called a trigger) is a bit out of the ordinary and the picture is humorous, you almost can't help noticing when it appears. The trigger that I use in many of my keynote speeches is the word *Hogwash!* Here is my definition of "Hogwash":

Hog-wash |hóg-wòsh| *n. 1.* A gut reaction that someone is manipulating you for his or her own gain, or feeding you a line of bull in order to deceive you (e.g., *I'll just borrow your password for a short time*); *2.* healthy skepticism that persists until the person requesting information from you proves he or she is worthy of your trust (e.g., *Until you prove to me that you actually need my Social Security number, I think you are full of hogwash*).
Synonyms: baloney, malarkey, nonsense, horse manure, prove-it-to-me

---

When the word "Hogwash" pops into your head, picture a pig feeding at a trough. Better yet, picture the person who is requesting your information feeding at a trough. The image is what makes it fun and memorable, so don't be afraid to be silly—it works. As the person provides legitimate reasons for needing the information, and adequate reassurance that your data will be handled securely, you can let him or her begin to rise from the trough. But don't let the person out yet, because social engineers are masters at using your natural biases against you.

Overcoming Emotional Biases That Cloud Our Reactions

Like Pavlov's dogs, which followed their owner's directions in exchange for doggy biscuits, we humans have been preconditioned to give our private information away in exchange for short-term rewards. We have been desensitized to the value of our data. We give it away to access social networks, win contests, download free software or music, gain access to websites, receive discounts, avoid confrontation, gain convenience, earn points . . . . As we add to our pile of doggy biscuits, we weaken the strength of our privacy.

Social engineers, con artists, and identity thieves employ a common set of phrases time and again to extract information from unsuspecting victims. Once you begin to tune in to these manipulative phrases (shown in *italics* in the following list) and detect the emotional biases they arouse (shown in **bold**), you will learn to more easily spot how and when you are being engineered out of your data:

1. *Trust me* . . . **Trust Bias:** We have a tendency to suspend our momentary skepticism (the correct instinct) and trust people (short-sighted) when they ask for our trust directly. We think, "Surely they must be legitimate if they are courageous enough to ask me for it." Anytime someone asks directly for your trust, "Hogwash it" (think Hogwash, picture Hogwash, and don't trust anyone until you've cleared the Hogwash).
2. *It's for your safety* . . . **Security Bias:** Someone asserts that what he or she is doing is for the "sake of security." Just like the Trust Bias, the social engineer is removing any doubt of legitimacy by "naming the evil." You think: "If someone is acting on behalf of my security, he or she couldn't possibly be a fraud. He or she wouldn't just bring it up!" Hogwash! That's why these social engineers bring it up—they know exactly how your brain has been trained to react ("Thanks for making me safe . . ."). In some cases, they are legitimate; in others, they might

be playing the role of the "double-agent." If someone involved with your identity uses the words "security," "fraud," "safety," "help," or any other term that is meant to make you feel like he or she is doing you a great service, *be suspicious*. The person is probably either committing the fraud or selling you something.

For example, when a computer technician calls your office and starts requesting information about your computers for the sake of security or to help you avoid fraud, you should turn up the volume on your observation power.

3. *We need to hurry . . .* **Rush Bias:** Someone rushes you through the decision-making process by telling you about a negative consequence if you don't act quickly. Con artists do this so that you don't have time to think about the decision you are making. If you ever feel rushed into divulging information, stop and think, "Hogwash!" Reveal sensitive information *only* as you become comfortable with the situation and the person.

4. *If you do this, I'll give you . . .* **Bribe Bias:** Someone wants to give you a gift in exchange for your information. The precondition operating here is that too many of us undervalue our personal data and consequently exchange it for impulse-based rewards that are of lesser value but satisfy a short-term desire. To combat this, recognize, and protect, the monetary value of your information. The individual pieces of your identity are as valuable as the assets connected to them. Your Social Security number can be attached to your credit rating, your home, your retirement benefits, unemployment, and more. As my father taught me at a young age, at least in the business world, there is no such thing as a free lunch. If you are getting something, you are giving something.

For example, when someone offers you a 10 percent discount on your purchase if you sign up for the company's credit card, calculate how much you will be saving in exchange for granting access to your credit history, address, telephone number, and so on. This may be a legitimate company, but the alarm should sound anyway to protect you initially from identity creep, not immediate identity theft. If you are purchasing $200 worth of clothing, ask yourself whether the $20 discount is worth one more company having access to your information—or possibly many companies, if the information is subsequently sold.

5. *If you don't do this, then . . .* **Fear Bias:** Someone threatens to take away your privileges or rights of access if you don't comply with his or her request, perhaps threatening to close, suspend, or cancel your account.

   For example, if you receive an e-mail that threatens to close or suspend your account if you don't comply with the enclosed request for information, red flags should appear and you should suspect a scam. No profit-driven, reputable company wants to lose your business, especially if you are a good customer. If you suspect the e-mail *might* be legitimate, confirm this with the company by phone, or visit your account on the company website.

6. *I need your help . . .* **Distress Bias:** Attackers will often pose as someone needing help because it lowers your defenses. You think: "How could they mean me harm if they are asking for my help?"

   For example, this is how "Friends in Distress" scams work on social networking sites. You believe that a friend of yours is appealing for help (e.g., usually asking you to send money), when actually it is a thief who has taken over your friend's account for the purpose of permanently separating you from your savings.

7. *Sharing one piece of data won't hurt . . .* **Slippery Slope Bias:** You think: "Giving this small piece of information, by itself, can't hurt me." But it's not a single piece of information that puts us at risk. It's the accumulation of data over time that puts us in danger.

8. *Do I need to speak with your supervisor . . .* **Authority Bias:** Don't question people who should know more than I do or have more power or status than I do. This derivative of the Fear Bias purposely leverages any lack of confidence you have regarding your superiors. Tell them they are welcome to speak to your superiors.

9. *I'm important . . .* **Flattery Bias:** Sharing information or access makes me feel important (I'm an expert). We all want to be in control of something, and con artists are all too ready to give us that control (in exchange for something).

10. *I just need a little bit of your information . . .* **Nonconfrontation Bias:** This is the most commonly used and most subtle of all of the social engineering tactics. Someone uses our discomfort with confrontation, our unwillingness to tell people no, and our fear of being disliked to manipulate us into giving out information that we would otherwise protect. We are so habituated into giving away our information that we

barely think twice when it happens. Part of this maneuver is to ask for innocuous, seemingly meaningless information first, to get you to let down your guard. Then, the thieves utilize the information "morsels" they have collected to appear believable and legitimate when they ask for further information (often, from another victim inside your company). In this way, they extract volumes of information without arousing your suspicion.

To be blunt, you must overcome your fear of confrontation—at least when it comes to protecting your identity. In instances of potential identity leakage, treat confrontation, saying no, and being disliked as the price of privacy. There are very few privileges that are worth having your identity stolen.

The more a social engineer can make his contact seem like business as usual, the more he allays suspicion. When people don't have a reason to be suspicious, it's easy for a social engineer to gain their trust.

—Kevin Mitnick and William Simon, The Art of Deception

Additional Social Engineering Techniques

Keep your eyes open for these other social engineering techniques. Social engineers will often:

- Use **charm**. Social engineers present themselves as likeable, charming people. This is what enables them to make you feel good about giving away information you shouldn't. To protect yourself against this tact, think of charm as *C-harm* (see harm) any time you suspect you are being charmed for nefarious purposes. Chances are, if you are giving information away, you are being C-harmed.
- Impersonate someone who has access or **power** (e.g., a repairman, IT support, a manager, an executive assistant, an account manager, etc.)
- Lower your guard first with **flattery** ("You are *so* capable . . .").
- **Accumulate** important data over several conversations or sources.
- **Rush** you by simulating a "crisis" so that you neglect to think.
- Use **fear** to scare you into acting when you should be thinking.
- **Intimidate** you into backing down.
- Lower your self-esteem by demonstrating **superior authority**.

- **Assuage** your doubt by claiming that it (whatever "it" is) is for your own good.
- **Name-drop**, especially using names that carry authority (your boss or superior).
- **"Prime the pump"** by baiting you with accurate background data (gathered earlier).
- **Divert your attention** by starting the conversation with small talk, and closing with a memorable, totally unrelated story (our brain remembers the beginning and ending of a conversation, but tends to forget the middle).

The Response: Slow Down and Observe

When an outsider has access to your identity, your trigger should automatically activate without thinking about it. (Hogwash!) Your first response should be to heighten your level of *observation*. View the situation as a child would—with curiosity. You can even borrow from what we teach our children: to be more aware in dangerous situations—*stop*, *look*, and *listen*:

- *Stop* what you are doing. Reject the pressure or temptation to multitask in an attempt to be more efficient. Don't talk on your cell phone or think about the next item on your to-do list. Reject the assumption that faster is better. Slow down and be present only to what is happening around you right now. Don't answer questions, hand over forms, or type a response until you are comfortable with the situation.
- *Look*, really look, at the world around you. Take out your spyglass and be more critical. Is someone peering over your shoulder at the ATM or while you are entering a password into the computer? Does the ATM machine look like it usually does? Is someone hanging around your mailbox or looking at your purse? Does the document on your desk contain sensitive or confidential information? The best way to remind yourself to look is to stand where you are, with nothing else to do but look.
- *Listen* to what your instincts are telling you. Ask yourself if your identity is safe. Is there a change in the environment that makes you uneasy or uncertain? What is your gut saying? Would a spy give away this information? Is the benefit you are receiving worth the data you are sharing? Do you feel as if you shouldn't ask questions (which generally means you should)? Be a healthy skeptic—not paranoid, but aware—of anyone

who is requesting your identity. Act on your instincts, as James Woods did in the example at the start of the chapter.

Examples of Evaluating the Risk

The best way to learn to *observe* and *evaluate* situations more closely is to walk though several scenarios and implement the concepts as we go. With enough practice, this mind-set should become a habit, and no longer require conscious thought. In these examples, we will apply the skills of *trigger* (request for information), *reflex* (hogwash!), and *response* (stop, look, and listen).

I warn you that, at first, this approach may seem to you to be a bit paranoid. That's only because we are using it as an educational tool to develop good habits. Recall that when you learned math, you did so by understanding each step in the process independently, as opposed to someone saying, "Do math." Once you have completed this process a few times, I assure you it will become second nature and you won't have to think through or name the individual steps. Until that happens, though, we need to make the learning process a conscious effort.

Now let's begin with the scenarios.

Shoulder Surfers You approach an ATM (*trigger 1*) and pull out your wallet (*trigger 2*). You remove your debit card (*trigger 3*). Thanks to the three triggers, you can't help but think, "Hogwash!" (*reflex*), a humorous but helpful warning to put your guard up.

Your level of observation increases and you begin to evaluate the situation (*response*). You take a few seconds (*stop*) and check to see if anyone is watching over your shoulder to steal your PIN number (*look*). You examine the ATM machine to make sure that there aren't any devices (skimmers or cameras) that aren't normally there (*look*). You check for anything out of place or any people who shouldn't be there; your instincts tell you that you are safe (*listen*).

If you are still in doubt, you apply the techniques that you will learn in Chapter 9, "Interrogate the Enemy."

Credit Card Skimming You are in a restaurant having dinner with friends and are about to pay the check with a credit card (*trigger 1*). The waiter has to take your credit card to another part of the restaurant to run the charges and will therefore be alone with your identity (*trigger 2*). You are aware that this is one of the most popular ways for thieves to steal your identity (by skimming your information on a pocket scanner), so you think, "Hogwash!" (*reflex*).

You are uncertain about how to react (*respond*), because you worry that you might look foolish to your friends if you make a big deal out of letting your credit card disappear. You have several options:

- *Pay with cash.* Remember, the old-fashioned way of paying has absolutely zero identity creep. Pay with cash when you don't want to let your card out of your sight or don't want to share information that will ultimately be stored in a database and sold to other businesses (as I pointed out earlier, companies buy your credit card histories so that they can market other services to you. They know that if you like to eat at certain restaurants, you will also probably be interested in their products).
- *Keep your card in sight.* If the waiter stays in view, watch to make sure your card is safe. And even if someone thinks you look foolish, take comfort that your identity will be safe.
- *Pay at the counter.* Take your credit card up to the cashier and pay there. That way, your card will never be out of your sight (control).
- *Monitor the signs.* Despite all of our training, probably what most of us will still do is let our card disappear with the waiter. Breaking this dangerous habit seems to be particularly difficult for many of us; therefore, we need another way to protect our identity when our information is out of our control. We do this by having a backup plan—a way to protect ourselves when all else fails. By monitoring our credit card statements and setting up automatic account alerts, we will catch any fraudulent charges before any damage is done. Read Chapter 10, "Monitor the Signs," for full details.

Phishing E-mail Scams   You receive an e-mail from your bank (*trigger 1*) saying that your account information (*trigger 2*) is out of date and you need to click on the link (*trigger 3*) to make updates; your account will be cancelled if you don't comply (*trigger 4*). All of these contacts with your identity trigger you to think, "Hogwash!" Your instincts tell you that this is a legitimate request because it displays the bank's logo, and the link you are clicking has the website address of the bank on it. Regardless, you *evaluate* the request by applying these interrogation techniques (which you will learn more about in the next chapter):

- You were not the one to initiate the request and are therefore not in control of the situation. You have no idea of who will have access to this information, whether at the bank or elsewhere. You don't know what information you will be giving access to, as you haven't clicked on the link to find out. From your accumulated knowledge, you suspect that it will be fairly sensitive information, including account numbers and passwords.

- You ask yourself if it is really necessary to share the information in this way (necessity). Because you have been educated about phishing, you know there are other ways to verify whether your account is out of date. Therefore, you close your e-mail and log in to your bank account directly to check for alerts from the bank that your information is incorrect. There are none, so you visit the My Account page and confirm there that everything is up to date. Finally, you call the bank to ask (interrogate) what the e-mail was all about. You are told that it is a phishing scam and that you should ignore further requests.

Action Item Checklist: Evaluate the Risk

- [ ] Slow down, and learn to observe what is going on around you.
- [ ] React to requests for identity of any type with healthy skepticism.
- [ ] Think "Hogwash!" when anyone asks for access to your data.
- [ ] Look for the signs of social engineering (fear, rushing, bribery, flattery, trust, security).
- [ ] Stop, look, and listen when your hogwash reflex triggers.
- [ ] When in doubt, *interrogate the enemy* (see Chapter 9).

Business Relevance

As I mentioned, this chapter, "Evaluate the Risk," and the next one, "Interrogate the Enemy" are two parts of the same process. In pure business terms, these comprise the most important skills that your executives, managers, and employees must learn in order to effectively protect your organization's sensitive information. Why?

Because no matter how secure your computer systems, no matter how much physical security you deploy, *humans will always be your weakest links.* The tightest classification system, the most expensive software, the most secure safes are only as strong as the weakest link, which, again, is always the human factor. The more technological security you implement, the quicker data thieves will be to attempt to socially engineer those inside your company (or pose as an insider) to capture your data.

As I said before, there is no substitute for learning these skills in actuality, as it helps to experience the techniques firsthand. Lacking experiential training, there are some guidelines you can follow that will begin to minimize the impact of the human factor:

1. Raise the awareness of, first, your executives, then your managers, and finally your employees to the risks associated with mishandling private company information. Do this in person, not by distributing a privacy policy, which many people won't read.

2. Inform the entire staff that dishonest people are out to get your company's private information, whether in the form of customer records, employee files, trade secrets, or other intellectual capital. Your competitors and, more recently, other countries will pay high sums for such high-quality intelligence.

3. Communicate to your team the *emotional impact,* in addition to the technical fallout, on victims of ignoring these policies. You must connect this experience to real-life consequences.

4. Motivate the troops by sharing with them in detail the *consequences* of data theft, loss, or leakage. Communicate this in no uncertain terms (e.g., they could lose their job, their bonus, their raise, etc.).

5. Define the problem by telling employees exactly what information you are trying to *protect;* emphasize that just because someone seems to have insider knowledge of company processes, language, and intellectual property doesn't mean they have a legitimate need to know the information they are requesting.

6. Avoid using language such as "privacy policy" and "information security," as people tend to stop listening when language gets

(continued)

(*continued*)

    technical or bureaucratic. Speak in metaphorical terms, such as "need-to-know basis."

7. Prohibit the release of information such as internal phone numbers, which makes social engineering much easier.

8. Set up a *classification* system (*public, internal, confidential, top secret*) under which all internal information is, by default, considered to be, at minimum, confidential. This establishes clear guidelines that leave no room for interpretation and sets the tone for a Culture of Privacy.

9. Train employees to recognize and pay attention to: triggers, hogwash, emotional biases, and control, justify, options, and benefits (Chapter 9). These form the basis for recognizing and responding to social engineering. Conduct this training in a lighthearted but highly effective manner, to leave no question in employees' minds about what they are supposed to do when information is being requested from them.

10. Give your team the *authority* and *budget* to implement proper solutions; Band-Aids and short-term solutions are not enough.

11. Set up a clear *legitimacy verification process* for your employees to follow anytime someone requests sensitive information from them. This process should include verifying the requestor's employment status (e.g., was he or she terminated?).

9

The Sixth Mind-Set: Interrogate the Enemy

Spies often get information simply by asking for it. Unfortunately, it really is that simple. Fortunately, the same technique—asking the right questions—can stop them in their tracks.

Victim #8,113,903: Social Engineers Go Corporate

Not long after Dr. Yamitori shared her username on a handout at a medical conference, she received an invitation to become friends with Dr. Xavier on a social networking site built for the medical community. Dr. Yamitori had shared her impressions of the conference on the site, and Dr. Xavier had been taking note. Over the course of the next month, the two never communicated directly via the network; rather, they received regular updates and comments posted by the other doctors in the network.

On Friday afternoon at 2:00 PM, Dr. Xavier (Dr. X) posted a comment directly to Dr. Yamitori (Dr. Y). Dr. X explained that he was in the process of researching software packages for his office and, knowing from the conference that Dr. Y ran an efficient operation, wanted to find out what software she used to manage her patient files.

Dr. Y happened to be at her computer and responded immediately to the query. Because both were part of a doctor's network, and concluding that the questions were innocuous, Dr. Y shared that she used Patient Relation 10.0

(continued)

(*continued*)

and was very happy with it. Dr. X thanked her, asked no further questions, and concluded the thread somewhat abruptly.

At 2:06 PM, Dr. Y's assistant sent an internal instant message (the silent and preferred form of communication in the office) to her saying that Dr. Xavier was on hold and had a quick follow-up question to their online chat. When Dr. Y picked up, Dr. X apologized for any trouble he was causing, but said he had one last question and thought it was a "good excuse to meet in person." Dr. X then asked Dr. Y if she would mind sharing the name of the software technician from Patient Relation Software who had installed the package for her so that he could ask some technical questions. Dr. Y gladly told him that her contact at the software company was Kenneth, and gave him Kenneth's phone number.

On Monday morning, before most doctors are in their offices, Dr. X's accomplice called Dr. Y's office and reached the receptionist, Priscilla. He told her that his name was Terry, that he was from Patient Relation Software, and that he was filling in for Kenneth, who was out sick. After flattering her ("Dr. Y says you're the real brains of the operation"), Terry explained that he needed to make a critical security update (version 10.1) to Dr. Y's software system. If it didn't happen right away, he added, her system could be the one that allowed hackers access into patient files. Immediately, Priscilla felt personally responsible.

Because Kenneth was out sick, Terry explained, he didn't have the username and password to dial in to Dr. Y's server and make the changes. He told Priscilla that as soon as the changes were made, he would call her back and let her know so that she could change her password. It was critical, he said, to change it as soon as he called in order to maintain security. In fact, he added, he would just send her a message on the social networking site, if she told him her username. She shared that as well, thereby giving him access to all of her friends who filled a similar role at other medical offices.

Knowing that Patient Relation was in fact the software package her office used to track patient records, that they were currently using version 10.0, that Kenneth was the name of their regular technician, and that she didn't want to be responsible for a data breach, Priscilla never suspected she was being socially engineered into revealing highly sensitive information. She gave Terry her password and, thus, full access to more than 17,500 private patient records, including their Social Security numbers, insurance data, medical histories, and even blood types.

> *The average recovery cost of a breached medical record is $294[1] which put the data breach recovery costs at Dr. Y's office at an estimated $5.2 million. The average cost of training a medium-sized medical office to recognize and repel social engineering: less than $25,000. Return on investment: 195 percent*

Everyone is so vulnerable to social engineering attacks that a company's only effective defense is to educate and train your people, giving them the practice they need to spot a social engineer.

—*Kevin Mitnick (former social engineer) and William Simon, The Art of Deception*

Interrogate Mind-Set

Spies ask direct and aggressive questions to get answers. Most people are only too willing to share their vast knowledge on private matters. Effective questioning is such an essential and fundamental component of the *evaluation* process that it warrants its own chapter (refer back to Chapter 8).

Fostering an attitude of curiosity (or in the corporate world, a culture of curiosity) is the most powerful critical thinking skill to have in your arsenal to protect sensitive information. Employees who can think critically and ask the right questions regarding data privacy make up the fabric that supports a Culture of Privacy. Interrogation is the art of questioning someone thoroughly and assertively to verify intentions, identities, and facts.

Here are the questions to ask:

- Who's in control?
- Can I verify?
- What are my options?
- What are the benefits?

When spies need information, they ask for it. They "socially engineer," or con, their victims with a variety of tools (as we saw in Dr. Y's scenario). This chapter will help you learn to detect and repel those tools.

No man really becomes a fool until he stops asking questions.

—*Charles P. Steinmetz*

The primary tool for evaluating risk once your reflexes have been triggered (remember: *Hogwash!*) is to interrogate the person or institution asking for your information. I want to quickly point out that in this context interrogation does not refer to forceful or physically abusive questioning. I define interrogation here as *clear, aggressive questioning* used to establish whom you can trust, how far you can trust them, and with what information.

Sticking with the language of espionage, an *enemy* is anyone or anything (including a computer, fax machine, e-mail, letter, etc.) that *requests your information, information about someone you know, or information about your organization.* My intent here is not to make you confrontational or assume a warlike mind-set—that is taking the metaphor too far. Once you have established a trusted relationship, you are no longer in enemy territory.

The Four Phases of Interrogation: ConJOB

There are four phases of interrogation, and four corresponding questions, that, when implemented, effectively begin to expose most forms of fraud:

1. **Control:** Who is in *control* of this interaction?
2. **Justify:** Can the person requesting information *justify* his or her legitimacy?
3. **Options:** What *options* do I have, other than sharing the data?
4. **Benefits:** What are the *benefits* of the particular choice I'm making?

1. Control

Anytime you are approached for information, whether by a person, an e-mail or paper mail, a fax, survey, contest, computer, or other source, the first question to ask is one of yourself:

Who is in *control* of this interaction?

Are you the one who *initiated* the process, or was it started by someone else (potentially a thief)? Most cases of identity theft happen when an outsider initiates contact with you, not vice versa. The thief calls you on the phone, sends you an e-mail, visits you at home or work, or approaches you in a public space, real or virtual.

If you did not initiate the exchange of information, *you are not in control* and your risk of fraud skyrockets. Initiate or terminate, I say. If you didn't initiate the transfer, take back control by terminating the exchange until you know what your next step will be. It is imperative that you maintain tight control over what sensitive data you release, to whom and in what manner.

If Dr. Yamitori had asked herself who was in control of the exchange of information, the answer would have been Dr. Xavier, and that would have been her first red flag.

Follow-on questions that will help you establish, or regain, control include:

- Why do you need this information, and how will you use it?
- Can you show me your written policy detailing this request for information?
- Will this information be discarded when it is no longer needed? How?
- Who will have access to my information, and how will it be protected against unauthorized access and use?

Access

Part of effectively controlling information flow is to understand levels of access. Spies give out information only on a need-to-know basis. In other words, they differentiate by user and type of information. This is particularly important in a business setting, as vendors and third parties are often allowed access to records with even less need to know and fewer controls than would govern the information internally. Information lost to third parties results in a higher per-breached-record recovery rate, as you can clearly see in Figure 9.1.

Am I Allowing Access On a Need-to-Know Basis Only?

Public data is different from classified data, so your response will be influenced by how sensitive the data is that you are giving away. You will, for example, interrogate someone requesting a Social Security number far more aggressively than you would someone asking for a first name. And don't forget that spies are experts at accumulating small pieces of information over time—they may ask you for one piece of identity here, another there. So also be aware of how much access you give to any one source *over time*.

When you enter a contest by giving your name, address, and yearly income, literally hundreds of people will see that information. Your data is collected, combined with credit records (purchased from other sources), and

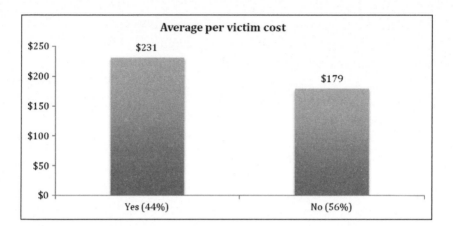

FIGURE 9.1 Did the Data Breach Involve a Third-party Flub?

Source: "Fourth Annual U.S. Cost of Data Breach Study," Ponemon Institute, 2009.

aggregated into a profile of who you are, what you are worth, and which products and services you might buy. Your information is not going to one person on the other end of the transaction; it is being sold to *anyone who is willing to pay to know more about you.*

When you mail a check, anyone with access to your mail has the potential to obtain your bank account number, name, address, and signature. When you post your phone number on a social networking site, anyone you have granted "friend" status to can see it, unless you have blocked it when you set up your permissions. In addition, you probably signed a contract with the social networking site (without knowing it when you accepted its terms and conditions) that allows the site to sell your private information.

In the case of Dr. Y's office, access didn't play a very prominent role until Priscilla was asked to share her computer login access. That was the red flag, though Dr. Y should have verified Dr. X's credentials earlier in the process.

He is educated who knows how to find out what he doesn't know.

—*George Simmel*

2. Justify

When someone else is controlling the flow of information, or to establish a higher level of trust, follow up with this question:

Can the person requesting this information *justify* (or verify) his or her legitimacy?

In other words, "Prove to me that you need it and deserve it." Can the person on the phone asking for your private information prove who he or she is and that he or she actually deserves the information? Companies spend good money assigning credentials to their employees.

> *The most common information that a social engineer wants from an employee, regardless of his ultimate goal, is the target's authentication credentials.*
>
> —Kevin Mitnick and William Simon, The Art of Deception

One of the easiest ways to spot a fraud is to verify these credentials *before* allowing access. Can these people prove their identity and their need to know the information? If it is a work situation, do you recognize their voice? Are they dialing from an internal number? Can they e-mail the request from a company e-mail? Will their superior verify the legitimacy of their request?

Most of us are vulnerable to social engineers because we are trained to trust first, ask later. This is an acceptable perspective when the stakes are noncritical. Ronald Regan had a signature phrase, especially when dealing with the Soviet Union: "Trust but verify." It is a translation of the Russian proverb, "Doveriai, no proveriai," and suggests that it is fine to extend trust, as long as you verify the worthiness of the party to whom you are giving it. But with information, which can be digitally copied and communicated in an instant, I contend that the proverb needs to be reversed to strengthen it:

Verify legitimacy *before* you trust others with sensitive information.

Priscilla could have easily justified whether to give the information to Terry by verifying his credentials (with a medical association or licensing body, or even with Dr. Yamatori, to find out whether she had verified he was trustworthy).

3. Options

Social engineers are counting on the chemicals in your brain (cortisol, generally) to override your common sense. When they put you in a state of panic, ask for your help, or flatter you, they know that your emotions are likely to override your logic and lead you to make rash decisions. When you interrupt this cycle and force yourself to think through your options, your brain has time to catch up and rationally evaluate the situation.

To slow down the interaction and remind your brain that there is more than one course of action you can take, ask:

What *options* do I have other than sharing the data or following the requestor's directions?

This is nothing more than a risk/reward analysis. Am I receiving something of equal or greater value for what I am giving? Can I give less than the person is asking, or nothing at all, and still receive the service he or she is promising? Remember, we have been preconditioned to think of our identity as less valuable than the assets to which it is connected.

Can you still receive the long-term benefit without giving the information? Will you still have an effective Facebook profile even if you don't share your birthdate? Could you pay the bill without sending a check through the mail? Will you still have a warranty on your refrigerator if you don't fill out the warranty survey card? In most cases, the answer is yes.

Five Advanced Interrogation Techniques

Interrogation is a form of regaining control over your information. When in doubt, ask more questions and explore more options. Here's how Priscilla could have done this with Terry, the bogus technician:

1. *Ask how.* How did you get my name and number? How do you know about our office? How do I know that you are who you say you are? This stall tactic gives you time to think, to listen for your hogwash response, and to evaluate the answers. If he is a fraud, he will be well practiced at answering questions of this sort. But as you continue to ask more detailed questions, fraudulent stories will begin to deteriorate.

2. *Bait him.* Feed him a piece of credible, but false, information to see if he takes the bait. For example, Priscilla could have said: "Oh, you are the one who filled in for Kenneth when he went on vacation last year, right? You've worked with Patty, our office manager before, haven't you?"

3. *Get proof.* Make him prove that he knows more about you or your company than he disclosed in the first conversation. For example: "Hey, can you tell me the last time I made a purchase on that credit card? How long has our office used this software? How many of our systems is your software installed on?" If he is a spy, he generally won't know any of the

real answers. When he hesitates or says that he doesn't know that information because he's not the "regular guy," tell him to ask his superiors and get back to you with an answer.

4. *Call back.* Take back control of the interaction by telling him that you need to give him a ring back. Say: "I've got to take another call. What's the number where I can give you a call back?" An identity thief will almost never give you a legitimate number (crime rings sometimes have temporary phone numbers). Or say: "Can I call you back using the number listed on my credit card [bank statement, phone book, etc.]?" When he says that he doesn't have a direct line, and will have to call you back, it's time to move on to more confrontational questions.

5. *Call the bluff.* Ask straight out: "Are you an identity thief? Let's assume you are an identity thief [chuckle]. How can you prove to me you are not? How can you prove to me that you are who you say you are? If I can't call you at the number I always use to call our tech support, why should I trust you? Why is your area code on my caller ID showing a different location from where you guys are based?" These types of questions tend to throw anyone off, so give the person a minute to recover. In espionage, this is called "requesting their bonafides"—proof that they are who they say they are. This is how spies keep from giving information to counterspies. You need to validate the person's information until you are comfortable that the person is legit.

Don't be afraid to ask more questions—as many as you need until you have no doubts about the person. Fraudulent stories tend to crumble about three or four questions deep.

Finally, don't be afraid to *say no*! Tell the person that you need to check on some things and will get back to him/her. Anyone who can't give you time to conduct due diligence is either a fraud or too high-strung to be dealing with.

4. Benefits

Your final question is:

What are the *benefits* of the particular choice I'm making? Do they *benefit* my lifestyle? Do they *benefit* my company?

You have to assess how the options you are evaluating fit into your lifestyle. Does it benefit the way you live? If it doesn't, you will quickly tire of the solution and stop implementing it. For example, if you buy a shredder and put it in your office even though you sometimes open your mail in the kitchen where there is no shredder, recognize that you probably won't walk to your office to shred every single document. More likely, you will make the excuse that throwing this one piece of identity in the trash won't cause problems. Over time, this will become your habit. So putting a shredder only in your office does not benefit your convenience-oriented lifestyle. Better to purchase two shredders so that you will continue implementing the solution.

As you probably noticed at the beginning of this section, the first letters of control, justify, option, and benefits form the acronym ConJOB. It has two purposes: (1) It's easy to remember and (2) it serves as a form of shorthand to help you remember the concepts involved in exposing a con job by using aggressive questioning.

Risk Scenarios: Practice Interrogating the Enemy

In the situations I provide in this section, assume that you have already observed and evaluated the situation but haven't yet been able to determine if you are at risk. Possibly your instinct is prompting you to inquire further. Interrogation is a perfect tool for situations that aren't black and white.

Scenario 1

You are buying a new car and plan to pay cash. The sales rep, Susan, asks for your Social Security number. What questions should you ask?

- Why do you need my Social Security number if I am not paying with credit?
- Can I still get the car without giving the number?
- Are you prepared to have me walk out on the sale if I don't give it to you?

If you are still not convinced that you should divulge your SSN, ask:

- May I speak with the owner of the business, please?
- Does the Better Business Bureau agree with your right to require this information?

In this situation, you are not preventing immediate identity theft. You are avoiding identity creep by giving out only the information that is absolutely necessary.

Scenario 2

A woman calls and says she is from your credit card company. She believes that your card is being used fraudulently and needs to ask you a couple of questions. Before you answer her questions, ask some of your own:

- May I ask more questions about why you need this information?
- Can you verify the last three purchases I made on my account?
- Can you tell me how long I have been a card member?
- May I give you a call back using the phone number on my credit card?

Scenario 3

Someone comes into your office wearing the standard uniform of your regular computer technician, but you don't recognize her. Still, she has a plausible story and asks for access to your server. In this case, ask:

- Weren't you guys just in here yesterday? (*Bait them.*)
- May I see your ID badge, please? (*Verify credentials.*)
- Can you hold on a minute while I call to verify your credentials? (*Slow down.*)
- Who within our company ordered the service call? (*Ask more questions.*)

Scenario 4

As you drive up to your ATM machine, you see a repairman there. He says that everything is ready to go; you just need to insert your card and get started. No questions needed here; just say politely, "No thank you," and find another ATM or go directly into the bank.

Action Item Checklist: Interrogate the Enemy

☐ Implement the four phases of interrogation by asking four revealing questions:
  - Who is in *control* of this interaction?
  - Can the person requesting the information *justify* his or her legitimacy?
  - What *options* do I have other than to share the data?
  - What are the *benefits* of the particular choice I am making?
☐ Implement the five interrogation techniques:
  - Ask everyone who requests data how they came to be in possession of any of your private information.
  - Bait them to see if they reveal themselves as untrustworthy.
  - Make them prove that they deserve the data.
  - Call them back on a published, dependable number.
  - Call their bluff by asking if they are an identity thief.
☐ Practice interrogating the enemy by expressing curiosity anytime someone has or wants your information.
☐ Don't be afraid to say no.

Business Relevance

From a business perspective, an automatic *privacy reflex* (**Hogwash**), *controlling the flow of information* (**control**), *verifying credentials* (**justify**) *and evaluating various alternatives* (**options and benefits**) are the fundamental concepts underlying a Culture of Privacy. This is really just a process of formalized awareness and inquiry about the origin, flow, storage, transmission, and destruction of your data in a non-technical manner. When taught correctly, data curiosity becomes a game—albeit, a high-stakes game. By the time your employees reach this point in the book (or in-person training), they should be prepared for and receptive to transitioning data privacy from their personal lives into their professional lives.

By likening it to a game, by couching it in terms of thinking like a spy, I am proposing a vastly different approach to the data security discussion from the norm. Generally, data theft and loss is dealt with only after the fact (after the breach occurs) and in a negative way (someone or some department is punished, admonished, improperly blamed, etc.). To create a constructive and preventative Culture of Privacy, securing a customer's Social Security number or the company's "secret recipe" must be a proactive and positive initiative. It should be a point of pride for each and every executive and employee to protect the company's assets, not just to fear the consequences of failing to do so. Fear, of course, plays a part, as it serves as a vital "smoke signal" for the instincts, but in a supporting role.

Imagine, if you will, the customer loyalty generated by a best-in-class company that treats customer data with the sanctity that it extends to the rest of the customer relationship. What if your company treated customer identity like Ritz-Carlton treats its customers? A Culture of Privacy is not an entirely separate initiative from other forms of strategy and marketing. It is the extension of those strategies, to include information protection. It is the ultimate recognition that *privacy means profit*. It might even provide differentiation and a competitive advantage as customer awareness of data safety increases.

Mike Spinney, a senior privacy analyst at the Ponemon Institute, provided an apt analogy in a recent blog post:[2]

> I was in an industrial facility recently and noticed large banners on the walls proclaiming, "12 Years without a Safety Incident." I also saw certificates honoring individual employees who had eclipsed certain thresholds without a time-lost safety event.
>
> It struck me that this is the kind of simple program that privacy and compliance officers can use as a model to create a "culture of privacy" throughout the entire employee community and instill a basic awareness of each employee's responsibility to protect sensitive information. Such programs would be relatively simple and inexpensive to implement because the model has already been used successfully for decades by safety officers to educate and reward employees for demonstrating effective safety practices in
> *(continued)*

(continued)
their jobs. A quick look around the organization reveals other programs that can be replicated by privacy and compliance officers. Human resources executives, for example, already offer training and awareness programs to prevent sexual harassment or various forms of discrimination.

Mr. Spinney goes on to suggest that it will probably take lawsuits like those already routine in the workplace arsenal (e.g., sexual harassment, safety violations, etc.) to give privacy the "teeth" accorded to other issues of workplace safety. Once again, we see the role of fear (costly lawsuits) reinforcing a proactive program of change (a positive Culture of Privacy).

10 The Seventh Mind-Set: Monitor the Signs

A s an added layer of protection, we must keep close tabs on the various red flags that indicate our identity may have been stolen. Generally, the best strategy is to catch identity theft in its earliest stages, before it becomes a more difficult problem to solve.

Over the past three years, stolen data that was subsequently used in *less than one week* jumped from 33 to 71 percent.[1] Clearly, identity thieves are counting on our lackadaisical attitude toward monitoring our wealth.

Victim #3,903,392: Friendly Fraud

Dixie's sister, Danny, came to live with her for the spring. Recently out of drug rehab, Danny didn't have a way to make ends meet and needed help getting back on her feet. Dixie, a deeply caring and religious person, decided to fill that role. Unfortunately, it didn't take Danny long to revert to her old habits.

Danny began using drugs almost immediately after her release, and steal-ing petty cash from Dixie's home that she believed would never be missed, to support her habit. This source quickly ran out, however, and because she was left alone while Dixie was at work, Danny had access to virtually every docu-ment and piece of information in the house. Dixie and her husband had taken no special preventative steps to protect their sensitive information, and Danny thought this was careless of them; more, she believed they were deliberately tempting her.

*(continued)*

(continued)

In April, Danny was able to look through the couple's tax documents, which had been left on the office desk waiting to be sealed and mailed. They contained all the information Danny needed to set up accounts on Dixie's credit without alerting Dixie what she was up to. And because they looked alike, it was simple for Danny to get a driver's license in Dixie's name. In short, Danny was able to fully adopt an alternate identity without being detected.

In most such cases, detection would have taken years, as all of the accounts that Danny set up were entirely new and covered by Dixie's spotless credit. But unbeknownst to Danny, Dixie had been monitoring her identity "vital signs," which fortunately would save her hours of recovery time. She had read an article in the newspaper about getting a free annual credit report from each of the three credit bureaus, and had ordered her first copy in May. She was curious to see what a credit report looked like. Imagine her surprise to learn how much money it looked like she had been spending!

Dixie alerted the credit bureaus the same day she received her first credit report, followed the guidelines put out by the Federal Trade Commission (FTC) for identity theft victims, and stopped her sister before she could make full use of her identity. Recovering her identity took less than 30 hours and cost her only $15 in notary fees.

Monitor Mind-Set

Spy networks monitor their assets (agents, information, safe houses) to detect trouble at the earliest stages. By monitoring indicators of breach or wrongdoing, they are able to contain information leakage before the damage becomes permanent. Correspondingly, by monitoring our identities (using either the latest technological tools or paper-based methods), we can detect fraud and stop identity theft before it causes permanent damage.

Tools for keeping track of your identity vital signs include identity theft monitoring services, credit report monitoring, balancing your checkbook, financial account alerts, and Social Security statement monitoring. At the organizational level, monitoring may include video surveillance, software footprint tracking, and tracking log files and key card access. But the most powerful form of monitoring at the corporate level is actually performed by your customers.

It is, of course, impossible to stop every form of identity theft. It is, however, realistic to catch theft before it becomes a major problem. The quicker you catch identity theft, the less time and money you will spend recovering from it. Prepare for the worst by having a backup plan—a way to detect fraud early in the game. *Monitor the signs!*

> *Over half of fraud cases are self-detected. Nearly 4 in 10 victims discovered the fraud while they were actively monitoring their accounts. Self-detection by electronic means [e-mail or Internet statements] resulted in lowest loss of money compared to other methods of detection. Victims who electronically monitored their accounts (either online banking or an ATM) accounted for the discovery of 15 percent of existing card fraud, and the fraud amounts for these detection methods are the lowest compared to any other means of discovery. [See Figure 10.1.]*
>
> —*"2009 Identity Fraud Survey Report,"*
> *Javelin Strategy & Research (p. 53)*

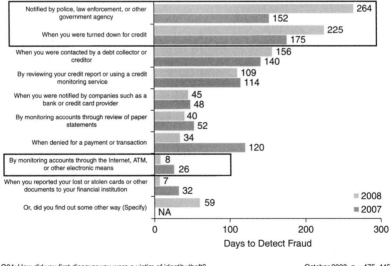

Q24: How did you first discover you were a victim of identity theft?
Was it by Q25: From the time the misuse of your information first
began, how long did it take you to discover it had been misused?

October 2008, n = 475, 445
Base: All victims
© 2009 Javelin Strategy & Research

FIGURE 10.1 How Fraud Was Detected and Length of Detection

Source: "Identity Fraud on the Rise But Consumer Costs Plummet as Protections Increase," Javelin Strategy & Research, January 2009.

It is just not possible to observe and ward off every threat to our identity. There will be documents that you forget to destroy or lock up, unused accounts that you neglect to cancel, checks that you continue to mail, and waiters you will allow to disappear with your credit card. Nor is it practical to believe that we can cover every situation that threatens the safety of our identity. Finally, there will always be some situations that are completely out of our control, such as data loss by large companies. Fortunately, we are not helpless, even in these situations.

Like experienced spies, we can institute a solid backup plan. It is extremely important to monitor the key components of our identities even as we eliminate, destroy, secure, lock, evaluate, and interrogate in every way possible. This plan is our safety valve, and once implemented, it is simple and effective to maintain. It starts with a *dossier* (French for "file"), which is nothing more than a collection of critical information on a single individual. It is like a report card on your credit identity. Unlike spies, who use dossiers to understand the people they are spying on, you will be collecting information on yourself.

Create a Dossier

Your dossier will comprise a collection of documents that are stored securely in your home or bank (see Chapter 7, "Lock the Docs") and that you regularly review and update. It is a paper summary of your identity as the outside world sees it (businesses, organizations, and government agencies). It is made up of several key documents: your credit report, bank and credit card statements, Social Security statement, wallet photocopies, and your password list. Virtually any of your vital documents could be included in your dossier, as well (birth certificates, marriage licenses, etc.).

A dossier has two purposes. First, it is *a place where you can quickly access a complete record of your vital information, in case your identity is stolen.* You will have the necessary account and phone numbers at hand to quickly cancel credit cards and bank accounts, and to file credit disputes.

Preparedness prevents peril.

—*Chinese proverb*

Second, by keeping the documents in a single place, you are able to compare them over time, to spot changes or inconsistencies. For example, if you review your previous credit history report against the latest version, you can quickly spot any changes that have occurred.

Build a dossier in the way that suits you best. Whether you use a three-ring binder, hanging file folders, or a large envelope doesn't matter. What is important is that you lock up your dossier in the safest way and place possible, to keep it from becoming a casualty of identity theft. The safest place is probably a bank safe deposit box or a waterproof safe that is mounted into the foundation of your home. If this sounds overly protective to you, keep in mind that many burglars target the documents or files in your home. As mentioned earlier, refer back to Chapter 7, "Lock the Docs," for more on this.

Monitor Your Credit Report Consistently

A credit report records a history of how you repay money you borrow from others. As I noted earlier in the book, there are currently three main credit bureaus in the United States: Equifax, Experian, and TransUnion. Credit bureaus track your credit history, generate credit scores, and produce credit reports—all for sale to other businesses. If you own a home, have a credit card, lease a car, or apply for or use credit of any sort, this information is reported to one, two, or all three of these credit bureaus. In addition, they collect information on how timely you pay your bills, how often you are tardy, how frequently your credit is checked by companies, and any changes of address, employment, or other personal information.

By monitoring these reports closely, you will know when someone else is using your credit file to their benefit. If an identity thief opens a new credit card or loan on your Social Security number, you will see it on your report. The quicker you spot the problem, the less trouble it will cause. Monitoring your credit report is one of the most effective tools for preventing minor identity theft from turning into full-scale identity fraud. It is very simple and takes only a few minutes to do, which may be why so many people tend to give in to their apathy and fail to follow through on this important task. Don't be one of them.

Order your credit report from the first of the three agencies. By law, you are entitled to one free report from each agency once a year. The easiest way to get a report is to visit www.AnnualCreditReport.com, or call 1–877–322–8228. Make sure that you request your free annual credit report from one credit agency only, as you will order the other two reports throughout the remainder of the year. By spreading the reports out over time, you will be monitoring your files consistently and frequently.

When your call or log on to the bureaus, have your account information handy. Even when applying for a free credit report online, you will often reach a screen that instructs you to call in to "confirm your identity." If you call, the representative will ask you a series of questions that range from your current and past addresses, bank and credit card account numbers, the date the accounts were opened or closed, your mother's maiden name, and date of birth. The rep may also ask you the amounts you have taken out in loans. Don't get discouraged by this process. This is just another way the bureaus protect your identity, ensuring they provide your credit information to only you and not an imposter.

Probably, your *evaluation* trigger is going off right now, and you are wondering why you should give out all of this information, given what I've been telling you so far. Good for you. Let me explain. There are two reasons: First, the three credit bureaus already have your personal information; they just want to verify (or authenticate) that it is really you requesting the report, not an impostor. So you are not sharing any new information with them. Second, the benefits (being able to monitor for signs of identity theft) outweigh the risks (sharing private information that isn't actually private to this particular vendor).

Skip ahead four months from today on your calendar and set up a recurring event that happens every four months (yes, that is how often you need to monitor your credit for fraud, and that is how often you can receive the reports for free). Again, to request and review your next credit report, go to www.AnnualCreditReport.com, or call 1–877–322–8228.

The second time you request your report, choose a different credit agency from the one you chose the first time (e.g., if you chose Equifax first, choose Experian second, TransUnion third, and return to Equifax one year from today). By month 12, you will be requesting the report from the same credit bureau from which you requested it the first time.

Ordering your credit report may not be the easiest or most hassle-free process, but it is *very effective* and *very inexpensive*.

What to Monitor

When you receive your first credit report, follow these steps:

1. Read through the *entire* report, including the definitions supplied by the credit reporting agency, to ensure that you understand how to interpret

the information. For a better understanding of how to interpret a credit report, visit www.Sileo.com/reading-credit-reports.

2. Review your report a second time, this time using a highlighter to mark any accounts that you don't recognize or that appear to contain inaccurate information (e.g., negative credit feedback where there should be none); use a different-colored highlighter to identify any accounts that you no longer need or use.

3. Contact the credit bureau regarding the accounts that you have highlighted, whether because you don't recognize them or because of erroneous information. Be aware that some company credit cards (like Sears) are issued by another company (e.g., GE Capital), so you may need to do some research on your credit card statements to figure out which company actually issued the cards. The credit bureau representative should be able to help you work through the questionable information. To reach a human being more quickly at the credit bureau, go through the fraud department, which has greater motivation to answer your call in a timely manner.

4. Call and cancel all of the accounts on your credit report that you no longer need or use. In this regard, please remember what I pointed out earlier in the book: *cancelling credit accounts could affect your credit score* (it could lower the amount of credit you have available), so do this only in conjunction with your accountant or financial counselor. If done over time, and in the right way, it won't adversely affect your credit score. When doing this, be sure to *call the company that issued the card or loan*, not the credit bureau. For example, if you have five credit cards that you no longer need (and probably have forgotten you even had), call each credit card company, settle any balances, and cancel the accounts. This is another means of *eliminating the source*. It minimizes the number of places that a thief can take advantage of your credit. If, on the other hand, you do not want to lose the credit value from those accounts, simply monitor them to make sure that no money is ever spent on them.

5. The next time you review your report, look for any changes against the previous report. If there are changes, verify that it is credit you applied for, and not a new account set up by an identity thief. You will probably have very little work to do on future versions of your credit report, as you will have done most of the hard work on the first round. Think of

the first review as a way to educate yourself about credit reports and to clean up the years of neglect and identity creep.

After you have completed the process yourself, encourage your spouse or partner to order and monitor their credit reports, which are mostly independent of yours. If you have children older than 16, I recommend that they monitor their credit reports as well, with your help. Review Figure 10.2 to see the differences between victims who detected identity theft themselves, versus those who were notified by an outside party, such as law enforcement or a credit card company.

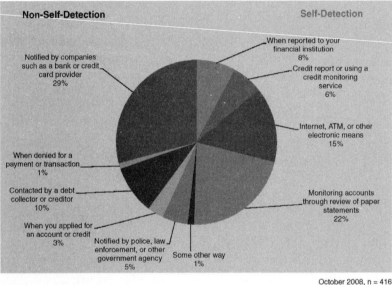

Q24; How did you first discover you were a victim of identity theft? Was it...

October 2008, n = 416
Base: All Fraud Victims
© 2009 Javelin Strategy & Research

FIGURE 10.2 How Victims Discovered Fraud (Self Detection vs. Detected by Others)

Source: "Identity Fraud on the Rise But Consumer Costs Plummet as Protections Increase," Javelin Strategy & Research, January 2009.

Identity Monitoring Services

To detect many types of identity fraud in the earliest stages (and thereby minimize further damage), you can subscribe to one of the identity monitoring services now offered by a host of providers. For a monthly or yearly fee, these services will notify you by e-mail of any changes or activity relating to your identity. Sorry to say that many of these services are a waste of money (they do what you can do for yourself, for free), but several of them are very well worth the investment (I use CSIdentity.com). The best of them provide the following features:

- *3-in-1 Credit Report Monitoring:* Includes credit inquiries, delinquencies, judgments and liens, bankruptcies, new loans, and more. The "3-in-1" means that the service monitors all three bureaus, Equifax, Experian, and TransUnion for changes in your report, not just one of them.
- *Court Record Monitoring:* Flags criminal actions associated with your name, birthdate, and/or Social Security number.
- *Public Record Monitoring:* Lists names and addresses affiliated with your Social Security number, address history, and any changes to same.
- *Noncredit Loan Monitoring:* Highlights short-term, high-interest payday loan activity that doesn't require a credit inquiry.
- *Internet Surveillance:* Monitors Web sites, chat rooms, and bulletin boards for illegal selling or trading of your personal information online.
- *Sex Offender Reports:* Alerts you to sex offenders residing in your zip code or moving in to your neighborhood, as well as any use of your identity by known offenders nationally.
- *Identity Theft Insurance:* Offers a $25,000 insurance policy, with $0 deductible.
- *Identity Theft Restoration Services:* Staffs full-service identity theft restoration experts to provide hands-on assistance to restore your credit and identity while you get on with your life. It is important that the monitoring service you are using provides this service "in house" so that they feel the need to take responsibility for your recovery in order to keep your business. Companies that outsource the restoration process tend to lose interest in you once you become a victim.

I recommend these services for everyone with a Social Security number, but especially for individuals who are too busy to regularly check their credit reports (which includes most of us, based on how few people consistently monitor their reports manually), who would like the peace of mind that comes from consistent monitoring, or who are already victims of identity theft. If you are among the latter, I can assure you that using one of these services is an easy way to track whether or not identity thieves are still taking advantage of your good name. These services have been invaluable in maintaining the health of my identity after I suffered several cases of identity theft. For recommendations on the best services, visit www.Sileo.com/ productreviews.

Many insurance companies also offer identity theft insurance as an endorsement on your homeowner's policy. This insurance tends to be relatively inexpensive and covers many of the fees associated with identity theft recovery. The biggest recovery expense is usually in legal fees, as you probably will need an attorney to help you recover your credit and fight any criminal actions. Every company's policy is slightly different, so make sure you understand which legal fees are covered and which are not.

Monitor Your Financial Transactions Effortlessly

There are four ways to monitor your financial transactions. I describe them in turn, according to effectiveness, from safest to most risky.

Account Alerts

Account alerts are the safest choice. Most credit card companies, banks, and investment firms allow you to set these up, and they comprise one of the most powerful methods for monitoring at your disposal—plus, they are completely free of charge. You generally set up account alerts by logging in to your online account (e.g., where you do your online banking, investing, etc.) and going into the alerts or notification section of the website. If you have trouble finding it, contact the financial institution and a representative will help you set up this feature.

Account alerts notify you automatically by e-mail or text message (to your cell phone) when a transaction is made on your account. For example, if you make a purchase on your credit card, an alert will automatically be sent to you detailing how much you spent, where you spent it, and on what date. The alert will also tell you when a payment is due or has not been received on time, or when private information has been changed on the account (often, a sign of fraud). Alerts are a simple way to keep track of credit card usage, bank transfers, low account balances, investment moves, and a handful of other helpful tasks, without doing any extra work. You just verify that each e-mail or text is legitimate. If it isn't, you call the financial institutions and inform them that you think you are the victim of fraud. They will help you handle it from there. By catching the signs early, you eliminate your liability and cost.

Online Statements

As you will see in Figure 10.3, the cost of the crime to the victim decreases substantially when the victim catches identity theft him- or herself (by effectively monitoring their paper or electronic statements). This is the second safest choice, because it isn't quite as convenient or timely as being alerted at the moment of the transaction (see below). If you aren't comfortable using, or don't want to receive, account alerts, consider monitoring your credit card, bank, and investment statements online. The key here is, the more often you monitor them, the more quickly you will detect foul play.

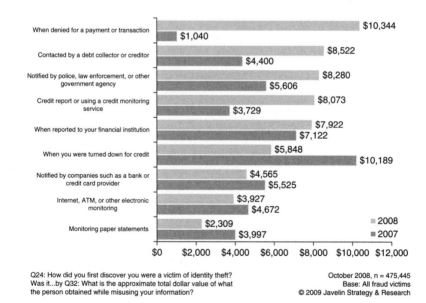

Q24: How did you first discover you were a victim of identity theft? Was it...by Q32: What is the approximate total dollar value of what the person obtained while misusing your information?

October 2008, n = 475,445
Base: All fraud victims
© 2009 Javelin Strategy & Research

FIGURE 10.3   How Fraud Was Detected and the Corresponding Recovery Costs

Source: "Identity Fraud on the Rise But Consumer Costs Plummet as Protections Increase," Javelin Strategy & Research, January 2009.

Using online statements offers two benefits. First, it eliminates paper statements from your mail. Second, because there is very little lag time between making a charge on your card and being able to view it online, you speed up detection time significantly. It's an excellent way to keep identity fraud from spinning out of control.

Mailed Statements

The third safest choice is to receive mailed statements. If you would rather receive paper bills or statements, follow this advice:

- Review them as soon as they arrive.
- Use an electronic calendar (like the one in Microsoft Outlook, Apple iCalendar or on your cell phone) to track your billing cycles. Most statements arrive at about the same time each month, so put a reminder in your calendar to watch for the statement in the mail.
- Use the recurring events feature in your electronic calendar to remind you of the statement every month. If the statement doesn't show up on time, call the company that issues the statement and ask when it was mailed.
- Review every transaction on the statement and make sure that you recognize where the charge is coming from and that the amount is correct or at least reasonable. Remember that identity thieves are usually smart enough to charge small amounts (or write small checks) each month, knowing they are harder to detect.
- If you find a discrepancy, immediately file a dispute with the credit card company or bank. If it turns out to be legitimate, you can always remove the dispute. In the meantime, protect yourself. You probably won't want to file your individual statements in your dossier (there would be too many), but it is a good place to file end-of-year statements and summaries.

Do Nothing

It hardly need be said that the riskiest choice is to ignore your statements and hope for the best. From my point of view, this is no choice at all. And one day, you will be sorry.

Monitor Your Annual Social Security Statement

Every year you should receive an account statement from the Social Security Administration. If you don't, you should contact them. The statement details your yearly earnings record, expected retirement benefits, and disability benefits. If your Social Security number has been stolen and someone is taking advantage of your benefits, you should be able to detect it by monitoring any changes in the statements. Do the following:

- Verify that your yearly Earnings Record on the statement matches your taxable income on your tax return.
- Verify that your benefits are increasing each year as you contribute more to retirement, not decreasing because someone is prematurely redeeming them.
- Encourage your spouse or partner to monitor his or her Social Security statement, as well, as it is completely independent of yours.

Keep these annual statements in your dossier or filed with that year's taxes.

Make Photocopies and Logs

In Chapter 4, "Eliminate the Source," I recommended that you make a copy of every piece of identity in your wallet. This copy should be stored in your dossier (which is kept securely in your home) and updated any time there are significant changes. These copies will enable you to quickly find and contact credit card companies, motor vehicle departments, banks, and other institutions if your wallet is lost or stolen.

As you opt out of marketing lists and information sharing, add the documents noting those changes to your dossier for future reference and verification. Keep a to-do list at the front of your dossier to track any future action items and the dates they need to be performed. For example, many of the opt-out programs stay in effect for only five years and so need to be renewed periodically. Write yourself a note on this page and include the date when you should renew your request.

Make a log of all of the important accounts, account numbers, login names, and passwords for each and every account you have. This should include bank accounts, brokerage accounts, insurance accounts, utilities and phone accounts, and any other financial institutions that require passwords or PIN numbers on their websites, phone systems, or ATMs. If your identity is stolen, you will have all of your account information in a convenient and safe place for quick access. It also provides a centralized place for your spouse or partner to find financial information if something should happen to you.

Action Item Checklist: Monitor the Signs

- ☐ Create a dossier.
- ☐ Order and monitor your credit report.
- ☐ Set up regular calendar reminders every four months to request your next credit report.
- ☐ Sign up for an identity monitoring service and identity theft insurance.
- ☐ Set up account alerts for bank, credit card, and investment accounts.
- ☐ Monitor your monthly statements.
- ☐ Use an electronic calendar (like Microsoft Outlook) to track your billing cycles.
- ☐ Monitor your annual Social Security statement.
- ☐ Make photocopies and logs.

Business Relevance

Monitoring the signs is the most effective way for businesses to *minimize* the damage done by data breach or workplace identity theft. **The best people to monitor the signs of data theft are your customers.**

The best defense against identity fraud is a partnership with your customer: Half of all fraud is discovered by customers.

—"2009 Identity Fraud Survey Report,"
Javelin Strategy & Research

Seven Monitoring Tools Businesses Should Implement in Partnership with Customers

1. *Educate* your customers (and employees) to recognize the signs of identity theft at your company. The more they know, the quicker they will be able to detect fraud.
2. Encourage your customers to go paperless and monitor their accounts *online*, as this eliminates risky physical records, greatly speeds the detection process, and lowers the financial damage to all concerned.
3. Offer identity theft *monitoring* to your customers and employees (you might also consider subsidizing the cost), as this speeds detection of identity theft and lowers the costs. This function can be outsourced to an identity monitoring company.
4. Make sure that your systems detect and *notify* customers when they utilize inappropriate identifying information as their logins, passwords or PINs (SSNs, birthdates, etc.). Employ strict controls to verify address changes, as this is the most frequently used way to take over an account.
5. Offer e-mail or text *account alerts* that notify your customers of possible fraud (e.g., address changes, e-mail address changes, bank transactions, balance thresholds, foreign transactions, suspicious buying patterns, online or wire transfers, alert shutoff, etc.).
6. Give customers the tools to *define limits* and situations under which the transaction requires prior approval (e.g., no single bank transfer of greater than $1,000).
7. *Reward* your customers when they detect a problem. This promotes loyalty, reinforces their positive habits, and encourages them to forgive the fraud because you are taking active steps to minimize the effects.

Field Combat: Target the Enemy

No one starts a war—or rather, no one in his sense ought to do so—without first being clear in his mind *what he intends to achieve* by that war and how he intends to conduct it.

The first and most important rule to observe in order to accomplish these purposes is to *use our entire forces with the utmost energy*. Any moderation shown would leave us short of our aim.

The second rule is to *concentrate our power as much as possible* against that section where the chief blows are to be delivered and to incur disadvantages elsewhere, so that our chances of success may increase at the decisive point.

The third rule is *never to waste time*. Unless important advantages are to be gained from hesitation, it is necessary to set to work at once.

> —Carl von Clausewitz, *Principles of War*
> (Emphasis Added)

11

Deploy Targeting Strategies: Accumulate, Prioritize, and Adapt

In Part II, I presented the first seven mind-sets of *thinking like a spy*, to establish *what* we do to protect private data (eliminate, destroy, secure, lock, evaluate, interrogate, and monitor). In this part, I introduce *targeting strategies* to demonstrate *how* to go about applying those mind-sets in the most efficient (time-related) and effective (quality-related) manner possible.

The most lasting safety changes emerge from building layers of security organically, beginning with the most important steps first, then customizing them to your particular requirements. By *targeting the enemy* in this way, you will reap the maximum return on your investment.

Victory #1: Building a Culture of Privacy from the Ashes of Failure

Rather than illustrating the principles of this chapter with another case study of corporate data breach, I'd like to share the steps my executive team and I took (and continue to build upon) to protect our data inside a new professional speaking and training business. Incorporating what we've learned over the past five years, this case study is an accurate representation of how we have accumulated, prioritized, and adapted our privacy processes to build a successful Culture of Privacy.

Phase 1: Defining the Problem (Pinpointing Our Risk)

Our data breach was grounded in the human factor, a potential risk at so many businesses. Our problem was a people problem—in our case, one person. Doug, an insider (or double-agent, to apply the spy metaphor), took advantage of our trust to turn private information into his own profitable enterprise. Needless to say, after Doug was caught, left the business, and went to jail, we shed a certain amount of the risk—but only for the time being. It didn't account for minimizing that same risk going forward as we began to build a new business. Our most pressing task now was to redefine how we brought people into our circle of trust, including partners, employees, and vendors.

Phase 1, our first priority, quickly became about *adapting* our hiring process with data privacy in mind. All employees, current and future, would be screened according to a new process. We instituted detailed background checks, both criminally and financially, as well as character-based testing, to better understand our candidates. We verified and interviewed references—personal, professional, and educational—using a vigorous process to expose fraud, deceit, and dishonesty. We implemented privacy education, beginning during the interview process so that job applicants knew the standards to which they would be held. And we enacted a monitoring system (including continual background checking services) to automatically update us on the levels of trust we could extend to each individual inside the business. In short, over the course of about a year, we *accumulated* a robust process that enabled us to hire (employees and vendors) with privacy in mind.

Phase 2: Motivating/Engaging the Troops (Establishing Personal Buy-in)

All the members of our executive team had experienced the consequences of data breach and identity theft firsthand, so motivation was not much of an issue. All of us clearly understood that *privacy means profit* and that it was our responsibility to build privacy into our corporate vision. Many businesses that fail to implement a genuine Culture of Privacy skip this step; they don't recognize that motivating employees, executives, and vendors to maintain data privacy is an ongoing process, not a one-time fix.

Phase 3: Destroying the Data

We had years' worth of back records sitting in banking boxes on storeroom shelves: past invoices, employee records, tax documents, financials—you name it. To reduce the volume of data that we no longer needed or wanted to store, we hired an on-site shredding company to help us completely destroy these archives, rather than do it ourselves. We worked with the company's staff every step of the way to make sure we were in control of the destruction process and that it was carried out to our specifications.

Once the bulk of the data had been destroyed, we purchased Fellowes' shredders for *every desk* in the office. We found that if our employees couldn't access a shredder within two to three seconds of their desks, the documents had a far greater chance of being thrown out without being shredded. We also placed commercial-grade shredders next to the photocopiers and printers throughout the office so that any unneeded documents being handled in those areas could be shredded on the spot.

Finally, we instituted a reward and disciplinary process to ensure that shredding became a part of our culture, and not just a fad. First, we instituted trash audits, where I would personally dig through the trash to see if any sensitive documents were being thrown out intact. This alone demonstrated a level of commitment to privacy that started at the top of the company. A positive inspection (no data exposed) resulted in some form of reward (e.g., everyone goes home early with pay on Friday). A failed inspection was also dealt with in a positive way: additional privacy training. It didn't take long for everyone to figure out that paid leave was more rewarding than falling behind with work because they had to attend privacy training. Once everyone bought in to the culture, we adapted the program to a long-term reward system (no failed audits this year affects bonus levels, etc.).

Phase 4: Securing the Systems

Our immediate response to address the security of our electronic systems was to pull our servers offline (only allow access from within the office, not from outside via the Internet) while we identified our electronic risks and formulated a plan to eliminate or at least minimize them. We found this to be such an effective strategy for keeping hackers from penetrating our systems that we never fully reconnected our file servers to the Internet.

Instead, we *adapted* server security to fit our demands; specifically, we moved the two mission-critical applications to which we needed remote access onto a completely different server and protected it behind an extra-tight firewall. The firewall was configured to allow only certain computers (via MAC addressing and VPN) into the server through one port (allowing us to close risky ports commonly used in hacking attempts) and into the two aforementioned applications. We also implemented encryption on our servers, our computers, our sensitive e-mails, and the wireless network. We took extra precautions on protecting our wireless network since this is such an effective and unobtrusive way to break into a business's data systems. In addition to WPA2 and SSID Masking, we also implemented MAC addressing so that only specific computers had access to our network (all of these solutions are discussed in further detail in Chapter 6, "Secure the Systems").

Now, instead of needing just our IP to attempt a hack, a hacker would have to know 7 to 10 pieces of key information about our system to get in from the outside. Few of our employees even knew all of the pieces of this puzzle, which added tighter security against an inside job. Additionally, most of our critical customer and employee data never left our offices.

By *prioritizing* how we protected different levels of confidential data, we eliminated almost 90 percent of the identity that came in contact with the outside world. In other words, we lowered our immediate risk by 90 percent, with minimal investment.

In the process of *accumulating* these layers of technological security, we switched our workstations to an Apple OS X platform in order to minimize the chances of malware letting a hacker through our security net (Apple computers, while not immune to viruses, malware, etc., have a far lower share of the computer market, and therefore attract fewer hackers).[1] Our research had led us to conclude that the OS X platform was better suited to data privacy for our specific type of small business.

To protect ourselves against internal threats, we established four groups of user-level computer and document access: public, internal, confidential, and top secret.

Finally, we began to treat our laptops and mobile data devices with more respect (which you will learn more about in Chapter 13, "Protect Mobile Data").

Phase 5: Locking the Docs

Ours is a small office and we *adapted* effective document locking techniques to fit our size and culture. First of all, we installed a high-quality alarm system in our offices to discourage break-ins. We equipped every office with a locking filing cabinet and a locking office door. Executive offices also included a locking fire-resistant safe and digital storage unit for securing highly sensitive information.

We only occasionally have visitors to our office, so we don't require every classified-level document be locked up (this is an example of adapting best practices to the pragmatics of running a business). Consequently, public and internal documents may be in full view, unless someone is visiting our offices, in which case we attempt to file or remove internal documents if an outsider is going to be on site for an extended period of time. Confidential documents are locked up after use, remain with the party responsible for their safety, or are worked on only in an office with a locking door. The door is shut and locked when the office owner is not present. Top secret documents either stay with the individual responsible for their safety, or are locked up, period. Before a cleaning service or other outside vendor is given access to the office, we do a "data sweep" for all potentially sensitive documents, locking or disposing of them appropriately.

Most of our client contact takes place in a neutral space where no documents or computers are easily accessible. We often hold meetings in a nearby café, to minimize traffic through our offices. It's convenient, enjoyable, and safe.

In addition, we created an outdoor locking enclosure for our trash dumpsters to discourage dumpster diving (defined in Chapter 2). This is such a common and easy target for thieves that we felt we needed to minimize access to our garbage.

Phase 6: Social Engineering Training

Each of our employees and executives is highly attuned to spotting a scam. Through ongoing experiential training, this cumulative process ensures that everyone on the team recognizes new forms of fraud and theft before they even become part of the public consciousness. Once individuals have been trained to recognize the signs of fraud, trust their instinctive emotions that signal trouble, and implement the appropriate response to any request for information (hogwash!), the danger that social engineering will occur is much reduced.

We had to *adapt* our training to a special contingency—a riskier environment. A side effect of being in the business of training people to detect fraud is that you are also teaching them how to commit fraud without being detected (because the social engineers learn the tools just as well, or even better, than the honest students). Consequently, we often see our skills being used against us. This won't, of course, be the case for most people reading this book, but it is certainly a sign of what is to come. In other words, keep in mind that none of what you are learning is static. Your knowledge must evolve with time, as it does for criminals.

For example, the minute a social engineer knows that a company has trained its employees to be on the lookout for flattery, bribery, and charm techniques, he or she might instead use the opposite tools to their advantage. The point is, there will always be new tools of deception, which is why we implemented phase 7.

Phase 7: Ongoing Monitoring, Education, and Improvement

We now utilize independent, outside experts to monitor financials, employee records, system security, and privacy practices. This gives us an impartial and ongoing look at the health of our Culture of Privacy. We conduct regular training sessions and assessments of best practices for data security, and constantly update our technology, to stay as far ahead of the curve on identity theft and data breach as possible. We also provide personal identity theft monitoring services to our employees as a benefit so that they don't log sick time resolving their own experiences of this crime.

In conclusion, I want to say that not only are these privacy practices *profitable and beneficial to our business*, they are, simply, *the right things to do*.

Target the Enemy: Three Principles

Targeting the enemy breaks down into three simple principles:

1. *Accumulate* layers of data security over time, rather than all at once, to form a safety net of privacy.

2. *Prioritize* your efforts to focus first on protecting the most valuable data and eliminating the greatest sources of risk.
3. Adapt the seven mind-sets to the particular needs of your home or business, rather than applying it in a formulaic, one-size-fits-all way.

1. Accumulate

Spies collect data with a great deal of patience and focus. They typically begin by capturing a kernel of information then add to it over time, focusing on the most valuable data first. Each piece of data, by itself, may appear to be worthless; but taken as a whole, the identity profile that emerges is well worth the investment.

You can use this same strategy to protect your private information. By accumulating privacy in layers (and focusing on the most important measures first), you will build a strong, multidimensional defense against identity theft and data breach.

Continuously ask yourself this question: *What is the next data security step?*

Little strokes fell great oaks.

—*Benjamin Franklin, Poor Richard's Almanac*

Over time, we have been giving away our privacy, often without even realizing it. We commonly trade our personal information for access to website content (e.g., free downloads, social networking pages), the chance to win a contest (iPods, vacations), or to cash in on a one-time 10 percent discount at a clothing retailer. I call this slow and unnecessary leakage of our personal information *identity creep*, and the people who collect our data, *identity creeps* (also referred to throughout the book as spies and thieves). These creeps request our information in a subtle way, and because the immediate benefits we are offered seem substantial and, often, harmless, we overlook the downside—that we are gradually broadcasting our identity to those who shouldn't have it.

One source at a time, we must reverse our bad habits and guard information, rather than give it out thoughtlessly. Understandably, we cannot stop sharing our information entirely. What we must do instead is determine what to share and with whom; and that is where thinking like a spy can help. By adopting a mind-set of accumulation, you will begin regaining your privacy immediately, one step at a time. This incremental approach also keeps prevention from becoming an overwhelming task and reminds you to consider the risk any time your identity is involved.

2. Prioritize

Some data is more valuable than other data, meaning that accumulating layers of security shouldn't be a random process. You need to begin with the most important items first. Social Security numbers are much more valuable than phone numbers, for example. Likewise, some sources of data breach pose a greater risk than others. Laptop computers, because of their mobile nature, are at a higher risk of theft than stationary workstations or servers.

Every home and every business will have to differentiate one level of risk from the next. Your job is to prioritize how you systematically eliminate or minimize those risks. Chapters 4 through 10 on the first seven mind-sets are organized in the order in which you should apply them, in most situations. For example, you should always attempt to *eliminate the source* before you *destroy the data*. If you can't *eliminate* or *destroy*, then *secure*. And so on.

To circle back to where we started, this is the order in which you should attempt to prioritize your privacy protection:

1. Eliminate the source.
2. Destroy the data.
3. Secure the systems.
4. Lock the docs.
5. Evaluate the risk.
6. Interrogate the enemy.
7. Monitor the signs.

Prioritizing ensures that you spend time first on those items that will produce the highest degree of safety. Thanks to the power of accumulating privacy by priority, you can spend just a few minutes a day taking steps toward protecting your data and still make substantial progress over time. As I said before, prevention is not a one-time fix. I strongly discourage you from sitting down one weekend determined to regain control over your identity all at once, or call a meeting at which you attempt to solve the "security problem" in a single session. This approach will prove to be too daunting, and chances are you'll quit before you accomplish what you need to. Instead, your goal is to accumulate small pieces of change over many months, so that, in the end, you protect sensitive data in an enduring and effective way. Think about accumulating privacy as Benjamin Franklin did about saving money—put a little away every chance you get and, before long, you will have amassed a fortune.

The question to ask of yourself and your business colleagues at this juncture is: *What is the next step we can take to deliver the most bang for our security buck?*

Think about how we accumulate security *by priority* to protect our homes and families:

1. We move to a safe neighborhood (*eliminating a portion of the risk*).
2. We install deadbolts on the doors (*locking up our valuable assets*).
3. We install an alarm system (or get a dog) to alert us to intruders (*securing our "system"*).
4. We pay taxes to fund our local police department (*monitoring*).

Taken individually, the steps would be inadequate to give you true protection; but taken together, they form a safety net that greatly lowers your chances of theft. You may spend days or weeks implementing all of the solutions, but each step gives you greater safety.

On a personal level, *freezing your credit* is the highest-priority item for protecting yourself against identity theft. This is where you should begin your accumulation process. In business, the priorities change depending on the size, type, and nature of the business. The chart demonstrates the difference in where priorities should lie between Financial Institutions (FIs) and other types of businesses. Clearly, insider theft should be a top priority of non-financial companies. This also demonstrates the need to *adapt* these (or any) suggestions to your specific environment.

3. Adapt

None of the tools or suggestions provided in this book will work well for you if you don't take the time to *adapt them to your situation*. Solutions are most effective when they are customized to the particular needs of the individuals or businesses involved. Figure 11.1 demonstrates some of the common ways that data is compromised, but it is important to determine how your business varies from the norm.

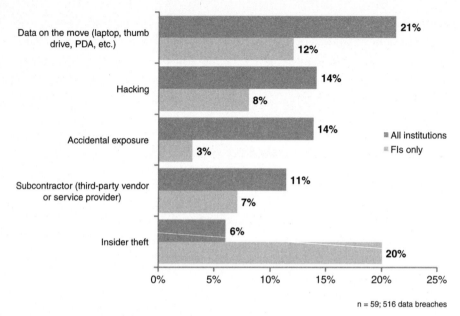

Q: How was the information breached?

FIGURE 11.1 How Sensitive Information Is Exposed

Source: Identity Theft Resource Center. Accessed September 30, 2008.

In the seven phases I and my colleagues went through to protect our business, we adapted the mind-sets to suit the design of our business:

- We invested little in motivation, as we had experienced the crime first-hand. We were already motivated and primed for action.
- We adapted our hiring and human resources processes to suit a small business, not a Fortune 500 company.
- Instead of spending vast resources on hardening our computer network to keep hackers out, we adapted the plan and took most of our sensitive information *offline*. This was a very nontraditional and highly effective modification.
- We have a low volume of traffic through our offices, so we invested more in keeping thieves out of our building (an excellent security system), opportunists out of our offices (locking doors), dumpster divers out of our trash (a locking dumpster enclosure), and war-drivers out of our airwaves (a highly encrypted wireless network).

- We are frequently the target of social engineering, therefore we adapted our training to include tighter protocols for controlling the flow of information and verifying the legitimacy of requestors. This is important to a business of any size.
- We are a small business and don't have the manpower for internal auditing, therefore we outsourced that function to people and businesses that have earned our trust over many years.

Action Items: Accumulate, Prioritize, and Adapt

To illustrate the changes in mind-set I have been recommending you work toward, here are examples of how you might cope with several high-risk identity theft scenarios before and after learning the seven mind-sets of a spy (including accumulate, prioritize, and adapt). Note that there is a natural overlap, or redundancy, between mind-sets, so that privacy may be approached from many directions. The seven mind-sets (as well as targeting techniques) appear in (**bold**).

Identity Exposure	Former Mind-set	Think Like a Spy Mind-set
Someone reputable asks for your Social Security number (at home) or your computer login and password (at work).	You know that these are sensitive pieces of information, but don't want to embarrass yourself or slow things down, so you share the information.	Your identity is "in play," triggering a higher level of consciousness (**Evaluate**). You ask a series of pointed questions until you are comfortable with your level of safety (**Interrogate**). If sharing the information cannot be justified, you don't give it (**Eliminate**). If it is justified, you verify that your data will be used only for its intended purposes by monitoring it after the fact (**Monitor**).

(continued)

(continued)

Identity Exposure	Former Mind-set	Think Like a Spy Mind-set
A "friend" on your Facebook page says that he/she is in trouble and needs you to send money.	This is a very close friend, for whom you would do anything, so you mail him/her money.	While this isn't a case of your identity being stolen (it's a case of your friend's Facebook identity being taken over), your suspicions are triggered (**Evaluate**). Before you do anything else, you call your friend directly (**Adapt**) and ask him/her if he/she contacted your through Facebook and actually needs help (**Interrogate**). As you learn more about social networking fraud, you begin to apply what you've learned about phishing and malware attacks to this new medium of communication (**Adapt**). Since you utilize social networking in your corporation, you decide to train your employees on safe social networking at your next privacy meeting (**Prioritize and Accumulate**).
A credit card statement arrives in the mail.	You look it over quickly, pay the balance, and file it away.	You verify each transaction as legitimate (**Evaluate**). If you are uncertain, you call the credit card company and ask questions until you are satisfied (**Interrogate**). If the statement refers to a card that you no longer need

Identity Exposure	Former Mind-set	Think Like a Spy Mind-set
		or use, you cancel it (**Eliminate**) and then shred the document (**Destroy**). If it is a necessary piece of identity, you contact the company and request online statements to replace mailed statements (**Adapt**). You set up account alerts to notify you about any transaction problems (**Monitor**). Finally, you file it in a locked cabinet (**Lock**). You implement the same basic procedure for all financial statements that arrive in the mail and apply the same tools at your workplace (**Adapt**).
You sign up for a new credit card, personal or business.	You take no additional steps.	You opt out of the company's information-sharing policy and request that you not be sent convenience checks or marketing materials (**Eliminate**). You set up online statements instead of paper statements (**Secure**). You turn on account alerts to monitor for fraud (**Monitor**).
You receive an e-mail from one of your financial institutions (e.g., your bank) asking you to update account information.	You read it and potentially fill it out since it has your bank's logo and e-mail address on it.	You delete the e-mail (**Destroy**) and log in to your bank account directly to look for any online alerts or notices about the request. If you still have questions, or your instincts suggest fraud (**Evaluate**), you call the bank (**Interrogate**).

(continued)

(continued)

Identity Exposure	Former Mind-set	Think Like a Spy Mind-set
A department store offers a one-time 10 percent discount if you sign up for its credit card.	If you aren't in a rush and don't already have the store's card, you accept.	You perform a cost-benefit analysis: How much value will you receive by selling your personal information (**Evaluate**)? If it is worth it, you will profit from the sale of your identity. Unfortunately, it is rarely worth it in the long term (you get a one-time discount; the store gets data on you that can last a lifetime).
You notice customer data, sensitive intellectual property, or employee documents out in the open at work.	You are relieved that you are not the one legally liable for the safety of those documents. But you clean up your own desk because you know the personal consequences of being irresponsible.	You assess the level of risk that the theft of these sensitive documents would cause the business (**Define**) and either lock them up (**Lock**) or shred them (**Destroy**). You educate your staff on the *seven mind-sets* to protect the business's assets, including your employee information (**Accumulate, Prioritize, and Adapt**).
You have only a few minutes to take steps to protect your identity.	You think, "One little change won't make a difference anyway," so you do nothing.	You understand that taking even a single step is better than doing nothing (**Accumulate**) so you proceed to Chapter 16, "Prioritize Your Attack: The Privacy Calendar" to start accumulating changes by priority (**Prioritize**).

Business Relevance

Your business has a finite budget to protect private information. To maximize your return on investment, it is imperative that you *target the enemy*. You cannot possibly eliminate all sources of risk, so you must approach data privacy in a systematic way. Building a lasting Culture of Privacy takes time (which is why we accumulate changes over months or years), money (which is why we prioritize how we allocate resources to the cause), and active leadership (someone to adapt theory to reality). Figure 11.2 illustrates how businesses invest in data safety after a breach, which serves as a pretty good real-world indication of where businesses should be investing *before* the breach.

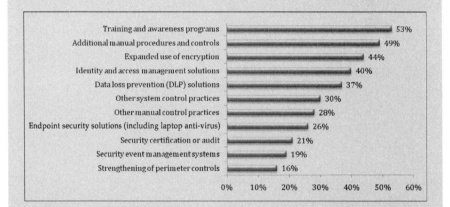

FIGURE 11.2 What Preventative Measures Have Been Implemented after the Data Breach?

Source: "Fourth Annual U.S. Cost of Data Breach Study," Ponemon Institute, 2009.

Clarity, flexibility, and longevity are what set successful privacy initiatives apart from those that fail. According to the Ponemon Institute, more than 88 percent of all data breach cases in 2008 involved insider negligence.[2] Implementing security that sticks on a gradual basis is more effective than attempting to make every employee read and follow a lengthy privacy policy in one fell swoop. Target these changes first:

(continued)

(continued)

- *Motivation:* Make privacy personal. Employees need to know that protecting the company's data is as important to the health of the business as protecting personal data is to their well-being. Make sure they understand that their jobs depend on data privacy.
- *Education:* Train employees on breach awareness, social engineering, and how to use preventative tools. At least 88 percent of this problem involves human error or negligence. As you can see from the chart on the previous page, the first step breached companies take is to properly train their executives and employees.
- *Definition:* It is imperative to know what information is at risk and where it lives inside your organization, both physically and digitally. According to the "2008 Global State of Information Security Study," published by Javelin Research, ". . . 71% of respondents say their organization does not have an accurate inventory of where personal data for employees and customers is stored."[3]
- *Protect Mobile Data:* Read Chapter 13 on locking down laptops and other mobile devices.
- *Encryption:* Encrypt every digital device utilized to receive, store, or transmit information or identity (laptops, wireless, backups, e-mail, etc.). According to the Identity Theft Resource Center's "2009 Breach Report," out of 498 breaches, only 6 companies reported that they had either encryption or other strong security features in place to protect the exposed data.[4]
- *Insider Theft:* Perform thorough background checks to weed out dishonest employees *before* they join your organization. Don't stop doing these character checks when your employees start work, either; many crimes are committed after people have been hired.
- *Shred:* Install high-quality shredders in locations convenient to all employees.
- *Classification:* Implement a classification scheme (physical and digital tiered user-access levels) and hold people accountable.
- *Elimination:* Where possible, stop using personal identifying information on mailers, forms, and the like. At a minimum, use accepted

methods of truncation and redaction to mask your customers' or employees' personal data.

"C-level executives believe the cost savings from investing in a data protection program of $16 million is substantially higher than the extrapolated value of data protection spending of $3.7 million. This suggests a very healthy ROI for data protection programs."[5]

In other words, the average ROI for data security spending, according to the "Ponemon Business Case for Data Protection Report" is approximately 332 percent.[6]

The next three chapters discuss in greater detail ways to target several of the most pressing and current sources of data breach and identity theft. For suggestions on ways to motivate, educate, and train your employees, and increase their awareness of how to accumulate, prioritize, and adapt to the ever-changing world of privacy, visit www.Sileo.com/training.

12 Defend Online Identity: Social Networking and the Cloud

Among the latest and most potent tools that enable fraud are the vast collections of personal information we accumulate, centralize, and share with the world in Web 2.0 applications like Facebook, Twitter, MySpace, LinkedIn, YouTube, Flickr, wikis, blogs, and other social networking sites. Protecting your identity doesn't stop at your computer; good privacy habits must extend into the online world.

Defend Mind-set

Spy networks build dossiers on their subjects until they know enough to manipulate and exploit them. As explained in Chapter 10, "Monitor the Signs," a dossier is simply a comprehensive collection of personal and professional information on a particular person. When we share that same information on a social network, even if it is only with "friends," or when we insecurely store that data on someone else's servers ("in the cloud"), we have effectively done the legwork for them.

There is no more appropriate place to apply the seven mind-sets of a spy than when sharing information about yourself on the Internet. Unfortunately, no matter how hard you try, you will never be fully in *control* of your information nor be able to accurately *verify* how your information is being used after it is stored and being managed on someone else's servers.

Before you share information online about yourself or your workplace, ask yourself this question: *What would the consequences be if this information fell into the hands of my worst enemy or competitor?*

Facebook, and social networking sites in general, are in an awkward stage of development, between infancy and maturity—capable in some ways, helpless in others. Lurking on the darker side of sites like Facebook, LinkedIn, and Twitter are scammers and identity thieves, who drool at the sight of what to them is an unchecked data playground. In contrast, most social networkers have become committed to all of the friendships they are creating and renewing.

There is no denying that Facebook and other social networking sites have a very luring appeal, as well as a great deal of functionality. From the comfort of your own home you can engage in a thriving social life. You can look up old friends, make new ones, build business relationships, and create a profile for yourself that highlights only your talents and adventures and leaves out all your flaws and troubles. If you are a businessperson, you can take the pulse of your customers on these sites, and find out what they want from your company. It is easy to understand why the number of Facebook users has skyrocketed from 1 million to more than 300 million worldwide in just over five years.[1] The speed of this tremendous social network growth helps explain why safety on these sites is still so immature: they have grown too fast for security technologies to keep up.

That said, Facebook isn't the problem; Twitter isn't the problem. True, they and other sites like them share responsibility, but so do we. To some degree, *you and I are the problem.*

Unfortunately, most people dive headfirst into this world of social connectedness without thinking through the ramifications of divulging all their personal information, which then travels at warp speed through cyberspace. It's like being a guest at a worldwide cocktail party, full of fascinating new acquaintances and delicious new drinks. We can't possibly resist the cocktails because they are so fun and tempting—besides, *everyone* seems to be having one.

The downside? No one talks about the information hangover that comes from such overindulgence. No one likes to focus on the fact that what you put on the Internet *stays* on the Internet. Worse, it also travels: it might show up on the front page of the *Wall Street Journal*, on the desk of your local law enforcement officer, in the hands of a prospective employer, or in your supervisor's inbox. All the personal information you post on profiles—names, birthdates, children's and pet's names, photographs, (all common password reminders), addresses, opinions on your company, your friends, and your enemies—is on display in a one-stop shop for identity thieves. There it is, all in one neat little package, and all a scammer has to do to access it is become your "friend." Or, if you've left your profile open to the outside world, the thief doesn't even need to be your friend.

Social Networking's Secret Weapon: Trust

Social networks, to varying degrees, are based upon an underlying assumption of trust among interlinked members. When the posts and links come from friends or acquaintances, they appear to be more credible than a spam e-mail from a stranger. You are connecting, or socializing, with people who associate with a group whose members you tacitly trust in general—"friends," colleagues, classmates, and others. There is no way, however, to verify specifically who in those networks you really can trust. On the whole, networks consist of honest, genuine members; but as the adage goes, it takes only one bad apple to spoil the bunch.

> *People are used to receiving spam and malicious messages in their e-mail, but it is much less common on Facebook. They are lulled into a false sense of security [and community] and act unsafely as a result.*
>
> —*Graham Cluley, quoted in "5 Facebook Schemes That Threaten Your Privacy,"*
> *J. R. Raphael*, PC World, *February, 25, 2009*

When you get down to solutions, protecting your data depends upon maintaining as much *control* of that information as possible, and *verifying* who is using it and how it is being used. Social networking, in its current state, *does not provide either of those assurances*. You never fully understand who is on the other end of your digital communications.

Thirteen Hazards of Social Networking

The profile shown in Figure 12.1 is an example from a seemingly simple but highly complex social networking site. For the sake of this discussion, we'll assume this profile exists on Facebook, the most popular social networking site, with almost 350 million members at the time of writing. But it could be

Name: John H. Smith
Birthday: 01/02/1973
Current City: New Orleans, LA
Hometown: Abilene, TX
Employer: XYZ Pharmaceuticals
E-mail: John.H.Smith@XYZPharma.com
Phone #: 555–555–5555

FIGURE 12.1

About Me: I have a cat named Samuel. I've lived in the French Quarter of New Orleans for three years (love Mardi Gras) and currently work in research and development for a pharmaceutical company. I'm interested in friendships, relationships, and professional networking.

any social networking site. This profile is what the outside world sees, but it's *not* what an identity thief sees; he or she sees a world of financial opportunity.

In addition to using the data in your profile to defraud you, other risks exist in the social networking sphere, which have been adapted from mail, e-mail, fax, phone, and financial scams of all sorts. Not all of them constitute identity theft, but all of them can result in fraud:

1. *Profile Building:* An identity thief might already have certain pieces of your profile from another source (e.g., the last four digits of your Social Security number that he or she obtained from your trash, a payroll stub, a piece of mail, an e-mail). Your Facebook profile provides the missing pieces of information that enable him/her to fill in the gaps and take financial advantage of your identity. In other cases, social networks allow businesses (including the social network itself) to build profiles on whom you are connected to, which products you search, and what marketing information you provide (through "quizzes," contests, and surveys).

2. *Social Security Number Capture:* Congress allows the last four digits of a person's SSN to be used as identification on public documents. Knowing people's date of birth and the city in which they were born are effective keys for "unlocking" the remaining five digits of their Social Security numbers. In a study published in the journal *Proceedings of*

the National Academy of Sciences, researchers correctly predicted the first five digits of a person's Social Security number about 40 percent of the time, just by knowing his or her hometown and birthdate. Given just those two pieces of information, they could predict all nine digits of the individual's SSN 8.5 percent of the time in fewer than 1,000 attempts.[2] An article in *Information Week* presents the findings in terms of real life implications:

> The accuracy with which SSNs can be predicted in 100 attempts varies, based on the availability of online data and on the subject's date and place of birth, from 0.08% to over 10% for some states. Such odds may not seem particularly dangerous, but an attacker could easily use a computer program to guess and guess again, over and over. With 1,000 attempts, a SSN becomes as easy to crack as a 3-digit PIN. Among those born recently in small states, the researchers were able to predict SSNs with 60% accuracy after 1,000 attempts.[3]

Once a thief has your Social Security number and a few additional pieces of information, available from almost any social networking profile, obtaining credit or services in your name is relatively simple.

3. *Password Hacking:* By using something obvious such as your dog's name as your password for the e-mail address you list on a social networking site, you facilitate an e-mail account takeover. Most people use only one or two passwords across all websites for each account they have. The personal information you input on Facebook may be the same that you use as your password or password reminder (mother's maiden name, birth city, pet's name, favorite sports team, etc.).

4. *Social Engineering:* The best way to socially engineer people is to first obtain enough information about them to make it look as if they can trust you. When someone is familiar with the most personal aspects of our lives, we tend to let down our guard. Remember Dr. X from the case study in Chapter 9, "Interrogate the Enemy"? It is an excellent example of how identity thieves use a social networking profile as a beachhead for launching a full-scale social engineering attack.

5. *Impersonation:* It is easy for a thief to become a virtual imposter of you when you have provided personal information, photos, and pertinent

facts about your life. Think about it: With all that identity in hand, what's to keep a thief from cloning your Facebook profile on another social networking site (like a class reunion site) and pretending to be you? Then, once he or she has "become you" virtually, the imposter can do anything he or she wants with/to your reputation. Social networks are not the only places where dishonest people can obtain this information; it's just the easiest and most comprehensive.

6. *Hijacked Profiles:* Account takeover is relatively common in the world of social networking. If, say, someone takes over one of your friend's accounts and then contacts you through the account to ask for money in an emergency, you have little way of knowing who is at the other end of the transaction. This is known as a "friend in distress" scam. Even though you appear to be in control of the interaction, you are not. Scammers have discovered that while your account might not be directly connected to money, it does provide enough information to enable them to steal from your friends.

7. *Malware:* Just as computer viruses and worms can be delivered through an e-mail or a website, they can also be delivered via social networking sites. Clicking on a link you don't recognize (or, all too often, one you do recognize but e-mailed by someone you can't trust) can lead to the download of software that gives hackers access into your system. Take, for example, the Koobface virus (the word "Facebook" rearranged), which infected PCs after users clicked on an enticing link that appeared to be from a friend. Once your computer is infected, the virus starts sending messages or wall postings to all of your friends and contacts, directing them to "a scandalous video of a mutual friend" or an equally enticing link. Anyone who clicks on the link in turn infects their own machines, further propagating the virus.

8. *Misleading Quizzes:* When someone invites you to take a survey ("10 Things Others Don't Know About You," "My Favorite Things," to name just two), beware! These are usually designed to harvest your data, not share yourself with others. When they ask you the name of your childhood pet, or cities you've lived in, they are usually looking for clues to your passwords.

9. *Malicious Widgets:* Most social networking sites allow you to install third-party applications to increase the functionality of the site. Unfortunately, several of these applications were designed with evil

intentions, such as to harvest your personal information. Currently, Facebook does not approve applications before making them available on the site, so there is no general control over quality. Some time ago, a widget named Secret Crush, which circulated widely, installed spyware on the computers of the unsuspecting, rather than helping them connect with virtual admirers, as promised.

10. *Phishing:* Most of us are by now familiar with phishing requests that arrive in our e-mail asking us to click on a link to update some form of personal information, and then deposit us at a website that looks like a legitimate page but is used to collect our data for sale on the black market. We are less prepared for similar requests that come via a wall post or direct message inside Facebook or that seems to be from Facebook itself, asking us to log in to accept its new privacy terms. When we attempt to log in, the thieves use the information to take over our account. By studying our profiles, cybercriminals can pretend to be from genuine organizations with which we affiliate (because we have listed those connections on our profiles), making phishing a customized endeavor.

11. *False Communities:* Anyone can form a group on a social networking site. But how do you know that the group you just joined wasn't built for the purpose of harvesting your information and then marketing to you or, worse, defrauding you?

12. *Malvertisements:* These are malicious advertisements designed to defraud you, collect your precious data, or install malware on your system.

13. *Breach:* How does your social networking site protect your profile and posting data? Is it susceptible to bots such as ZombieSmiles that allow hackers into your Facebook profile through the site's own client interface? Every computer system is theoretically penetrable. Think about what would happen if everything you've posted on Facebook were to go public.

Almost any scheme that can be enacted via older forms of media (e-mail, fax, phone, website, in-person) can be carried out via newer media (social networks, blogs, instant messaging, text messaging, photo sharing, video sharing, wikis, etc.). You also need to know that social networking sites don't exist just for the purpose of connecting individuals to like-minded people. They are building profiles on you so as to sell your information to others and market products and services to you. Most important to keep in mind, though, is the one factor that makes social networking sites a more effective fraud tool than all the others: *trust.*

> No matter how many privacy options the site offers . . . it's hard to escape the fact that information sharing is what makes Facebook users valuable to marketers. And the company has a powerful financial incentive to discourage its users from becoming too private.
>
> —*Martin Kaste, NPR News, January 4, 2010*

Ten Steps to Safer Facebooking

The good news is that most social networks operate similarly, so once you have learned how to protect your information on one site, such as Facebook, it is easy to replicate on others (assuming they provide the same security and privacy tools). To that end, in this section, I provide 10 steps to take on Facebook to protect your identity, which you can then adapt to other social network sites.

1. *Limit access:* If they are not your friends, don't pretend. Don't accept friend requests unless you are absolutely sure you know who they are and that you would associate with them in person. Yes, it's flattering to have a lot of friends, but it also increases your exposure to dishonest elements; it may also become overwhelming and annoying to receive communications you don't actually care to accept.

2. *Limit exposure:* Don't join every social networking site, and don't allow just anyone to become your friend. Choose one or two sites that suit your needs, are well respected, and show social respect for you by providing privacy controls to protect you and notifying you that they exist. Then, *share limited amounts of information.* Be cautious about the personal information that you post on any social networking site, as there is every chance in the world that it could spread beyond your original submission. It may be fun to think that an old flame might find and contact you; it's less fun to think about the scammers and thieves now clammering to access that personal information as well. Think twice about discussing your pet, or sharing your date of birth,

current home address, e-mail address, or cell phone number. Remember, what you share becomes public information. And if you also use any of those details as part of a username, password, or password reminder, be doubly sure to keep it *secure* and off social networks.

3. *Secure privacy settings:* According to "The Privacy Jungle: On the Market for Data Protection in Social Networks," "Despite signing up being considered legal acceptance of the Privacy Policy in every site studied, only 5 of the 29 general-purpose sites required actively checking a box to indicate acknowledgment of the privacy policy . . . [and] very few sites encouraged users to read it."[4] Facebook actually does a good job of explaining how to lock down your privacy (and, by default, is starting to require you to pay attention to privacy settings). To make it easy for you, follow these steps:

   a. Spend 10 minutes reading the Facebook Privacy Policy (or the privacy policy for the social network you are joining). Doing so is an education in social networking privacy issues. Once you have read through even one privacy policy, you will never again view your private information in the same way. As you read, look for answers to these questions: Does the site own any information that you publish there, including posts, photos, videos, and so on? If not, does the site have unlimited rights to copy, publish, or reproduce it? (It probably does, as this is what gives these sites license to publish this information in the first place.)

   b. Visit the Facebook Privacy Help Page, which has a wealth of information—*if* you take the time to read it. It explains how to minimize all possible personal information leaks, which you should have read about in the privacy policy. Once you understand how to do this on one social networking site, it should become automatic on most of the others.

   c. Customize your Facebook Privacy Settings to suit your needs; specifically, you want to confirm that only the information you want shared is shared. This simple step will reduce your risk of identity theft dramatically. Items to leave out: your real birthday, address, or phone number.

4. *Exclude unwanted outsiders:* First, modify your privacy settings so that search engines can't index your posts and photos. Unless you want all of your personal information cataloged by Google and other search

engines, you have to restrict your profile so that it is not visible to these data-mining experts. At the better social networking sites, you can set this in the privacy settings. Second, limit the number of add-on applications you allow to access your Facebook profile. The more applications and, therefore, individuals that have access to your data, the greater the chance it will be stolen.

5. *Be wary of quizzes, surveys, and causes:* Many Facebook quizzes and causes are used to harvest your private information for marketing or theft purposes. *When you agree to take a quiz or join a cause, you are also agreeing to give that program access to your account and your information.* A popular quiz currently making the rounds on social networking sites was designed to assign you a ficticious "adult movie" (i.e., porn star) pseudonym. It asks for your very first pet's name and either the street you grew up on or your mother's maiden name, which happen to be three of the most common password reminder questions. Again, it is in your best interest to give Facebook and the applications on Facebook as little information as possible. As security technology matures, these will once again become safe and useful tools, but until then, protect yourself.

6. *Click wisely:* What may look like a status update or message from a friend, with a cool new video attached, could be a phishing attack that will lure you to a fake website and trick you into revealing personal details and passwords. And as I've warned previously, if you receive a post requesting money to help out a friend, do the smart thing and call the friend in person. Thieves use "friend in distress" schemes to take over someone else's account and then make a plea for financial help to all the victim's friends (who think that the post is coming from the victim). As with all matters of identity, verify the source.

7. *Remember the first law of social networking: Posting is public.* Seemingly obvious, this precaution is constantly overlooked. When you post (I use the term "post" to encompass tweeting, blogging, commenting, writing on a wall, publishing to a website, and certain types of texting, instant messaging, etc.), you are making the information available to everyone on the Internet (unless you somehow restrict access). Compare this concept to in-person relationships, which are often much more discreet.

For example, you wouldn't tell your boss about the successful job interview you just had at another company, whereas you probably would tell your sister or best friend. But when you post this type of item online, you are collapsing those layers of distinction, or access, down to a one-dimensional view, where everyone has equal and identical access to your job news, whether you wish it or not. Denying, ignoring, or misunderstanding this basic principle of social networking—that posting is public and will be seen by others—is what leads teenagers to populate MySpace with pictures and content that they would never want their future employers, college admissions officers, or parents, to see. To date, it has already led to the derailing of mergers, the scrapping of highly confidential marketing strategies, and the firing of employees.

8. *Learn the second law of social networking: Posting is permanent.* When you post, you are producing a permanent piece of digital DNA that, for all practical purposes, never disappears. Your words, photos, and videos are forwarded, replicated, backed up, and quoted, hence become a permanent part of the Internet firmament. In other words, before you post, ask yourself if you're willing to claim ownership of the piece for the rest of your life. It is very hard to think a week in advance, let alone 20 years.

9. *Know the third law of social networking: Posts are exploitable.* Whether they are used against you in a court of law (yes, posts have been treated as admissible evidence), corrupted by identity thieves and social engineers, or aggregated by companies that want to sell you something, posts can and will be used in ways that the average user is not currently considering. Once again, ask yourself what your worst enemy, your ex-spouse, or your chief competitor might do with the information you are sharing.

Without question, social media and social networking are killer apps, and are here for the long term; they fulfill too deep a need in our lives and are too profitable for businesses to write off as a passing trend. But their efficiencies and benefits are not reasons to ignore the safety features that can help protect you against their just-as-real disadvantages. Neglecting to follow these steps is like refusing to wear a seatbelt when you get in your car.

10. *Maintain a healthy skepticism of social networking:* Apply the hogwash mind-set to *every* piece of information you share on the Internet, topped with an additional dose of skepticism. Social networking sites

are currently fraud hot spots, and being aware of this reality will take you a long way toward preventing a data breach hangover.

E-mail

Protect your e-mail address just as you would your home address. As your e-mail address becomes more public, you receive more spam (junk e-mail). Eventually, one of the spam e-mails will be realistic enough to trick you into entering information you shouldn't. Approximately 94 percent of all e-mails received are considered spam,[5] and while most are just marketing offers, some contain spyware, viruses, and malicious links that attack your computer and allow access to your personal information. Here are a few points to remember:

- Set your e-mail privacy and spam controls high.
- Never reply to a spam e-mail, even to request being removed.
- Research links before you click, including clickable images.
- Don't trust offers that seem too good to be true.
- Never enter personal or financial information into pop-up windows.

Google

What started in 1997 as a research project and mission to organize the world's information has turned into the world's largest search engine.[6] Google has given anyone with an Internet connection access to more information than they ever imagined was possible. With such quick access to so much data, you need to be careful what you put on the World Wide Web.

Have you ever searched your name in Google? You might be surprised to find information about yourself that you had no idea was out there—and that you wish wasn't. For example, a crime you committed in your younger years, and that you were told had been expunged from your record, may still turn up on Google. How is this possible? The most common way is through newspaper articles that have been archived on the Internet and are easy to access with a simple search. Remember, *posts are permanent.*

Here are a few privacy issues to keep in mind when it comes to Google:

Google's Cookie and Toolbar: Each time you use the Google search engine, the program automatically inserts a self-renewing cookie with a unique

ID number on your hard disk. As you surf websites, Google records your activity and saves your searches. The advanced features on Google's new toolbar for Internet Explorer not only update automatically, but also track which websites you visit. There are, however, ways to change your Internet options to stop cookie tracking; to learn more about this, visit www.google.com/support/accounts. Remember, *nothing you do on the Internet is private*; it is all tracked, aggregated, analyzed, sold, and used for a variety of purposes (many of them good).

Google Maps and Google Earth: Google acquired Keyhole in 2004 and, in 2005, turned what was called EarthViewer 3D into Google Earth.[7] This program has been criticized as constituting an invasion of privacy and a threat to national security, as it gives any individual the ability not only to look up your address but also to see an actual street view. Although a few high-security locations have been pixilated out of Google Earth, this program essentially gives individuals the ability to point and zoom in on any location in the world. Combine this with "geo-tagging," and you have a disaster waiting to happen. An example of geo-tagging is when you take a digital photo and it captures your physical location as part of the photo data (iPhones do this automatically). Then, when you upload it to, say, your Facebook or Flickr profile, anyone in the world can map where you are, versus where you live. You have just given a potential thief the tools to track your movements while you're on vacation. Even simpler, websites like FourSquare.com and other location-based social networking sites make your physical location available to everyone.

Google Mail: Google's mail service, or Gmail, offers users free webmail. Upon sign-up, most users notice right away the targeted ads that appear on the right side and above their e-mail listing. According to Google's privacy page, "Google believes that showing relevant advertising offers more value to users than displaying random pop-ups or untargeted banner ads. In Gmail, users will see text ads and links to related pages that are relevant to the content of their messages. . . . No e-mail content or other personally identifiable information is ever shared with advertisers."[8] Although Google may not be sharing the content of your e-mail messages directly with advertisers, the messages are being scanned for content, and populated with relevant advertising. Most people and businesses probably don't consider an e-mail that has been scanned by others to be truly private.

Google Docs: Google Docs is an amazingly powerful platform that essentially replaces Microsoft's Office on your computer. It has many advantages: It is considerably less expensive, is always up to date, and is available from any computer connected to the Internet. It also gives you a level of freedom to work on your computer, share, and collaborate that is not possible when your documents are available only on a physical hard disk. Google Docs is rapidly being adopted as the office suite of choice by government agencies, educational systems, and businesses. But as with any web-based application, there are privacy concerns. For further details, read the Business Relevance box at the end of this chapter.

Google's profit model is based on collecting, indexing, and sharing as much information as possible about everyone who uses its suite of tools. Because Google dominates the search engine market, websites, businesses, and individuals are highly dependent on it. This dependency, unfortunately, makes us more likely to overlook privacy issues with the company (e.g., "Gmail is so useful, I couldn't live without it, even though I know I'm foregoing some of my privacy"). I'm not suggesting that the solution is to stop using Google, the Internet, or web-based tools. What I am saying is, be aware and discriminating when you use these tools.

Action Item Checklist: Defend Online Identity

☐ Know what information about you is on the World Wide Web. Google your name, phone number, address, e-mail address, and any other personal information you are curious about.
☐ Leave out all these identity pieces when building your social networking profile:
- Date of birth
- Address
- Phone number(s)
- Any password reminders you use (high school, city born, pet's name, etc.)

(continued)

(*continued*)

☐ Read and understand your privacy settings in Facebook, Twitter, LinkedIn, MySpace, and other social networking sites; adjust them to protect your identity information.

☐ Vary your passwords online and make them more complex (see Chapter 6, "Secure the Systems").

☐ Be alert to and wary of "friends in distress" scams, posted links, and other social engineering scams.

☐ Only "friend" your actual friends

☐ Understand both the benefits and drawbacks of responding to quizzes and surveys, and utilizing widgets, groups, and third-party applications, before you add them.

☐ Don't forget that *posts are permanent, public, and exploitable.*

☐ Protect your e-mail by:
- Setting your e-mail privacy and spam controls high.
- Never replying to a spam e-mail, even to request being removed.
- Researching links before you click, including clickable images.
- Not trusting offers that seem too good to be true.
- Never entering personal or financial information into pop-up windows.

☐ Become knowledgeable about Google search engines, cookies, and the Google toolbar. Extend what you learn to other search engines and websites.

☐ Read, understand, and adjust your privacy settings in Google, Google Docs, Gmail, Hotmail, Yahoo!, or other online accounts.

Business Relevance

Defending online identity is rapidly becoming the most overlooked privacy issue facing corporations big and small, even though it has the potential to be the most devastating. The issue isn't limited to employees and executives using social networking in unauthorized or damaging ways to the corporation. Social networking is, in fact, a subset of a larger computing trend called "cloud computing."

Because the average individual is familiar with social networking, it is an easy way to communicate the benefits and drawbacks of cloud computing with employees and executives. Simply put, when you teach your employees to understand the risks of social networking, you are also educating them on the fundamental risks associated with social networking's more complex relative: public cloud computing. Both computing trends bring to the forefront a single question: *Who controls your data?*

To help answer that, read this succinct definition of cloud computing provided by the World Privacy Forum:

> For present purposes, cloud computing involves the sharing or storage by users of their own information on remote servers owned or operated by others and accessed through the Internet or other connections.[9]

In other words, cloud computing is the outsourcing of your computer processing, storage, data backup, or applications—your computer server in the sky, protected or not. Here, I am referring to public cloud computing, where the services are available to the general public. Private cloud computing, where a corporation builds an internal cloud that cannot be accessed by the public, has different privacy and data security concerns.

Examples of prominent public cloud computing platforms include:

Productivity Applications: Google Docs, Google Calendar, Gmail, Yahoo!Mail, Hotmail

Off-site Backup and Sharing: iBackup, @Backup, Xdisk, DataProtector, DropBox

Vertical Applications: Salesforce.com, Quickbooks Online

Social Networking: Facebook, LinkedIn, MySpace

Blogging: Wordpress, Typepad, Blogger

Micro-Blogging: Twitter, Facebook Status Updates, LinkedIn Status Updates

Photo Sharing: Flickr, Photobucket, Picasa, SmugMug, Yahoo! Photos, Facebook

Video Sharing: YouTube, 12Seconds, Viddler, Facebook

(continued)

(*continued*)

The advantages of cloud computing are significant:

- *Cost*. You get all the power of an application developed for a large corporation at a small fraction of the cost. You pay only for what you use.
- *Scalability*. Adding users is simple, even when they are in multiple locations.
- *Automation*. Software upgrades, hardware maintenance, and connectivity issues are handled by the cloud service, lightening the burden on your technical staff.
- *Reliability*. Computing in the cloud increases your service levels to that of a corporation, meaning less downtime for system or network issues.
- *Mobility*. Data available in the cloud is generally accessible from anywhere you have an Internet connection and a web browser.
- *Redundancy*. Your data is generally backed up by the cloud service provider, providing you off-site data redundancy should problems arise.
- *Collaboration*. Sharing data and tracking changes is easy when it is centralized and accessible from any Internet connection.

The disadvantages of cloud computing have not yet been fully cataloged or understood, but a list of data privacy concerns assembled by the World Privacy Forum include:

- *Ownership*. In many cases, it is unclear who owns the data stored on external servers. Many cloud service providers do not address this issue. Others claim ownership of the data when you agree to use their services (but they bury this distinction in legalese). Still others maintain the right to copy, use, change, publish, display, distribute, and share with affiliates or the outside world what you have placed in the cloud, again burying the details in a legal contract that the average user never reads (have you read Facebook's or Google Docs' privacy policy?). In other words, you no longer have strict control over what happens to your data. Data ownership becomes even more obscure when the cloud provider:

- Is a blind subsidiary of a competitor, a government agency, a foreign agency, or an Internet news service.
- Is sold to another company (along with your data).
- Goes bankrupt (and its assets—your data—are sold for transfer of assets).
- Merges with or is acquired by another company (adopting the new company's terms of service).
- Modifies its terms of service to its advantage (which you agree to simply by visiting the website).
- Terminates your contract (without providing you a copy of your data).

From a personal standpoint, photos of your children could legally end up in a national advertising campaign without your consent (the provider owns the photo or, at least, the rights to the photo). From a corporate standpoint, the secret recipe or intellectual property you detail in a Word document backed up on a cloud-based storage site is no longer clearly your sole property.

> For example, a trade secret shared with a cloud provider may lose some of its legal protections. When a person stores information with a third party (including a cloud computing provider), the information may have fewer or weaker privacy protections than when the information remains only in the possession of the person. Government agencies and private litigants may be able to obtain information from a third party more easily than from the original owner or creator of the content.[10]

> The World Privacy Forum also states:

> The more activity that a user conducts in the cloud, the greater the risk of third-party disclosure. Consider the user who employs a cloud provider to provide a complete backup for the user's hard disk. The provider would, in essence, maintain a full record of the user's computer activities. Anyone seeking access from the provider might obtain all of the user's records. For

(continued)

(continued)

example, in a divorce, a lawyer for one party might seek useful information such as documents, videos, photographs, e-mail, and other data from the other party's cloud provider.[11]

- *Disclosure*. Regardless of ownership, what data can the person or business operating the server on which your data is stored disclose to others (third-party vendors, government agencies, suing parties, competitors) without your consent or notice?

  For information that would have otherwise been in the sole possession of a user, the transfer of the information to a cloud provider creates new opportunities for the information to end up in government hands without notice to the user and without the user having an opportunity to object. For many users, the loss of notice of a government demand for the data is a significant reduction in rights.[12]
  A private litigant or other party might seek records from a cloud provider rather than directly from a user because the cloud provider would not have the same motivation as the user to resist a subpoena or other demand.[13]

- *Location*. When you store data in the cloud, you cannot be certain of where your data lives. It could be stored in other countries or, more likely, in multiple locations.

  Any information stored in the cloud eventually ends up on a physical machine owned by a particular company or a person located in a specific country. That stored information may be subject to the laws of the country where the physical machine is located. For example, personal information that ends up maintained by a cloud provider in a European Union Member State could be subject permanently to European Union Privacy laws. . . . Information in the cloud may have more than one legal location at the same time, with differing legal consequences.[14]

- *Compliance*. Certain professions (doctors, lawyers, clergy, counselors, accountants) require that client data be handled in a certain way.

  For example, health record privacy laws may require a formal agreement before any sharing of records is lawful. Other privacy laws may flatly prohibit personal information sharing by some corporate or institutional users. Professional secrecy obligations, such as those imposed on lawyers, may not allow the sharing of client information. Sharing information with a cloud provider may undermine legally recognized evidentiary privileges.[15]

  Customers of tax preparers enjoy some statutory and regulatory privacy protections. These customer protections in turn limit the ability of a tax preparer to use a cloud provider.[16]

13 Protect Mobile Data: Laptop Responsibility

Why, you might wonder, does the subject of protecting laptop computers and mobile data devices warrant an entire chapter when I've already discussed laptop protection throughout the book? Part of the answer is profit-driven: Laptops are currently at the bull's-eye of *targeting the enemy* and, therefore, protecting your bottom line. No single information asset is targeted so consistently by thieves, compromised so frequently inside corporations, or reported on more vociferously by the media. Keeping customer records, employee data, and proprietary intellectual capital safe and secure is essential to running a profitable company. In other words, a data breach can easily destroy customer trust, stock value, brand reputation, and, on occasion, the business itself.

The second part of the answer lies in the fact that most of us can empathize with the experience of having a laptop stolen. Just the thought of your laptop being stolen, loaded with mission-critical and sensitive personal information, is enough to cause night terrors. Moreover, it turns out, most of us are very emotionally attached to our laptops; consequently, even the prospect of having them compromised (dare I say, violated?) elicits a protective response.

Because we treat laptops almost like an extended member of our families (we bring them on vacation, take them in for checkups, upgrade their capabilities, occasionally spend more time with them than our children), *laptops provide an excellent shortcut to stimulate data responsibility*. If we fail to protect them properly, they may become a major threat to the safety of important personal and professional information. Therefore, the laptop is an excellent privacy-training tool. Protecting this single repository of identity requires us to utilize all seven mind-sets plus the skills discussed in Chapter 11, "Deploy Targeting Strategies."

The laptop's greatest strength is its mobility; it's also its greatest weakness. According to the Privacy Rights Clearinghouse, the records of 250 million U.S. residents have been exposed to identity theft due to security breaches since 2005.[1] A 2009 study conducted by the Ponemon Institute sets the average cost per data breach at $6.75 million per reporting company; and the theft of a laptop or mobile data device accounts for 36 percent of reported data breaches.[2] I repeat: Laptops are at the bull's-eye of *targeting the enemy* (see Figure 13.1).

Employees and executives alike are the primary sources of data breach. While technology often enables the breach, it is generally a poor data-handling decision made by a company employee that is ultimately the root cause.

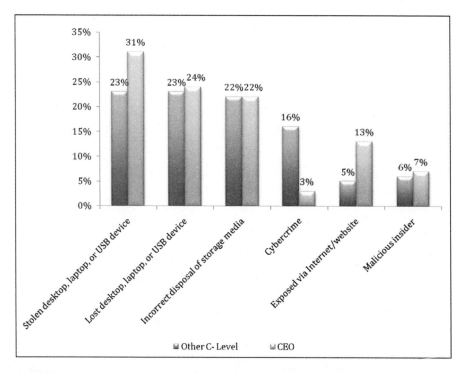

FIGURE 13.1   Sources of Greatest Risk to Sensitive Data

Source: "Fourth Annual U.S. Cost of Data Breach Study," Ponemon Institute, January 2009.

It is our responsibility as employees, executives, and individuals to understand the steps we can take to protect our mobile data devices, then take them. I define a mobile data device as any piece of equipment or medium that allows you to electronically store quantities of personal identification information (name, address, phone number(s), Social Security number, passwords, account numbers, important and confidential e-mails, etc.). Laptop computers, or laptops, are the most common of these devices to be breached, since their hard drives often carry vast quantities of identity data. (Note: I use the term "laptop" in this chapter to signify all the various mobile computing devices that currently exist, as well as new ones that are constantly being introduced, like the iPad.) Smart phones (e.g., BlackBerry, iPhone), PDAs (e.g., Palm), USB drives, CDs, DVDs, tape drives, and ordinary cell phones also qualify as mobile data devices.

The rest of this chapter is made up of a series of comprehensive checklists of your responsibilities regarding mobile data devices (all of which, for convenience here, I refer to as "laptops") and the corresponding *mind-sets* (shown in italics) to apply in protecting them. Although it is written from the perspective of the person responsible for the laptop, it can also serve as a framework for designing a companywide laptop privacy policy.

Mobile Data Device Responsibilities and Best Practices

Before employees can be expected to protect their laptops, the executive team must:

- *Define* what is at risk and the potential problems and consequences the business faces by mobilizing data.
- *Motivate* staff at all levels to follow security best practices.
- *Engage* your employees and executives in a Culture of Privacy by making an emotional connection to the cause (i.e., make it personal), utilizing a common language of understanding (e.g., think like a spy), and leading by example.
- *Prioritize* and *adapt* the following suggestions to maximize both your short- and long-term plans for *accumulating* mobile security.

Before you save sensitive data to the mobile device, it is your responsibility to:

- *Verify* acceptable use and alternative *options*:
  - Determine if your organization allows you to remove the data in question from the office in the first place. Do you have permission to save the desired database, Excel file, Word document, customer list, employee record, intellectual capital, financial statement, or marketing strategy, on your laptop, thumb drive, or other mobile device?
  - Decide if it is absolutely necessary to remove the file(s) from the more tightly controlled and secure environment of the office. In many of the major cases of reported data breach, the data stored on the mobile device did not actually need to be there in the first place.
  - Verify that you have been authorized by your supervisor to place a copy of the data on your device. When in doubt, check with your manager, supervisor, or privacy officer to determine the correct course of action.
  - Exhaust lower-risk *options* for accessing the data first. In many cases, it is possible to utilize a secure remote connection to access the data so that it never leaves the company premises. You lower your personal liability when you access the data through centralized, highly secure methods.

As you save sensitive data to the device, it is your responsibility to:

- *Control* exposure and *eliminate* unnecessary transport:
  - Minimize the number of records you transfer. If you don't need the entire contact database, take only the records that you need. In case of a breach, this minimizes exposure.
  - Minimize the corresponding fields for each record transferred. If you need only names and phone numbers, don't transfer additional account information such as addresses, account numbers, and so on.
  - Consider "de-identifying" the data, to render it anonymous. For example, if you track medical records using a Social Security number but are transferring the data to do a high-level analysis of overall profitability, there is no need to include the SSNs in your transfer. Exclude that column from the data you take with you.

Before you leave the office, it is your responsibility to:

- *Verify* that your system is digitally *secure:*
  - Attempt to encrypt the individual data file. In addition to encrypting the data device itself, it is possible in many software programs to encrypt the individual data file for an added layer of protection. This will protect the individual sensitive files with a separate, strong password.
  - Make sure your data device storage unit (e.g., hard drive, SIM card, SD memory card) has been encrypted. This will most often be the responsibility of your IT department, but it is your responsibility to verify that they have done their job.
  - Protect your device with a strong password that utilizes letters, numbers, symbols, and upper/lowercase characters, where possible. Keep your passwords separate from the computer itself.
  - Ensure that you have the proper tools to connect to a wireless network securely, as necessary.

Once you have left the office, it is your responsibility to:

- *Defend* your online communications:
  - Utilize a secure wireless Internet connection only (e.g., in airports, hotels, coffee shops, etc.). Make sure your IT department has enabled WPA2 wireless encryption on your wireless device and that you are utilizing a wireless access provider with strong encryption. See Chapter 6, "Secure the Systems," for more details. USB wireless sticks, which are the equivalent of adding a cell phone to your computer, tend to be more secure than the average wireless network. For a review of these devices, visit www.Sileo.com/productreviews.
  - Run a secure firewall between your laptop and your connection to the Internet.
  - Utilize SSL-encrypted e-mail or a proprietary e-mail encryption system. E-mail sensitive data only when absolutely necessary.
- *Lock* your laptop:
  - Physically secure (lock down) the device when in transit (e.g., in your car, at the airport, in your hotel room). Other attendees at a conference could be trustworthy or they could be foreign competitors looking for insider secrets.

- Utilize the safe in your hotel room. It's not a perfectly "safe" safe, but it is far better than the alternative.
- If there is no safe in your hotel room, hang the "Do Not Disturb" sign on your door and notify housekeeping that you will not be leaving the room and don't want to be bothered. This tends to keep extraneous people out of your room (though I have still had hotel employees access my room after I requested they not—the bed was made when I returned).
- *Keep the laptop on you.* Notice I say "on," not "with." While keeping it with you might seem safe, it rarely is. We tend to set things down for "just a minute," and that is all it takes for theft to happen. If you have it with you, have it *on* you. Utilize a backpack, messenger bag, or other carrying case that you can physically wear and that encourages you to keep it on your person until you reach your destination.
- Use one of the various locking and alarm devices that exist for laptops and mobile computing devices. They are not perfect, but they eliminate easy theft and might encourage a criminal to move on to an easier target. To learn more about these products, visit www.Sileo.com/ productreviews.
- *Monitor* your laptop:
  - Especially as you go through security at an airport, you must keep an eye on your laptop. Security checkpoints are a mass confusion of what belongs to whom. Don't put your laptop on the X-ray belt until you are ready to walk through the metal detector. Then follow it visually until you get to the other side of the X-ray machine. Laptops frequently disappear before their owners have made it through security.
  - Don't put your laptop down as you check in at the airport or your hotel or buy a cup of coffee. It takes only a fraction of a second to steal. Likewise, don't leave it in a conference or meeting room while you step out for a cup of coffee.
  - Utilize one of the LoJack-type software programs (or MobileMe for Apple Macbooks) to track your stolen computer once it connects to the Internet. Some of these security devices will also allow you to erase your hard drive remotely.

When you no longer need the sensitive data on your device, it is your responsibility to:

- *Destroy* the data:
  - Remove and electronically destroy all remnants of the sensitive files on your device (e.g., digital shredding, low-level formatting, and, occasionally, as in the case of DVDs, CDs, and tape backups, complete physical destruction). If this task falls under the responsibility of your IT department, it is your responsibility to make sure, to the best of your ability, that they do their job.

If your laptop has been stolen, it is your responsibility to:

- Report it to the local authorities.
- Report it to your company (if it is a company laptop or mobile device). Most likely, data breach notification laws will dictate how your company will respond to the loss of information.
- Alert anyone who might be affected. If it is your personal laptop, it is your responsibility to alert anyone whose data was stored on your computer. At the business level, those decisions should be made in conjunction with legal counsel.
- Take the proper precautions, if possible, to track your laptop or remotely erase the hard drive and mobile information (iPhone, BlackBerry), if you have software installed that allows you to do so.

Utilizing a laptop comes with a great deal of responsibility, as does handling any type of sensitive information. In an information economy that revolves around technology, our most valuable asset is the information we collect, store, transmit, and protect every day. As executives or employees of our respective organizations, not only is it profitable for us to protect sensitive information, it's also the right thing to do.

Action Item Checklist: Protect Mobile Data

- ☐ Know what is at risk on your mobile data devices.
- ☐ Verify acceptable use of your mobile data devices with your company.

❏ Control exposure and eliminate unnecessary transport of your mobile data devices.

❏ Verify that all of your systems are digitally secure:

- Encrypt individual data files, as well as your hard drive, SIM card, and SD memory card.
- Protect laptops and mobile devices with security software and strong passwords.

❏ Defend your online communications:

- Utilize a secure wireless Internet connection.
- Run a secure firewall.
- Utilize SSL-encrypted e-mail and e-mail sensitive data only when absolutely necessary.

❏ Physically secure your mobile device while in transit:

- When traveling, utilize the hotel room safe to store your mobile devices.
- Use a backpack or other carrying case to keep your mobile devices physically *on* you.
- Consider adding a locking or alarm device to your laptop and mobile computing devices.
- When going through security at the airport, don't put your laptop on the X-ray belt until you are ready to walk through the metal detector, so that you can keep an eye on it until you reach the other side.

❏ Utilize a LoJack-type software program to track your laptop if it is stolen.

❏ Destroy any sensitive files that you keep electronically after you are done using them.

❏ Take the proper recovery steps if your laptop or mobile device has been stolen.

- Report it to local authorities.
- Report it to your company.
- Alert anyone who may be affected.
- Track your laptop remotely, if possible.

Business Relevance

I have spent most of this book attempting to build a bridge between the worlds of personal data protection (to avoid identity theft) and professional privacy (to minimize data breach). The recurring theme is simple: good personal data habits instilled at a human level lead to good data privacy habits at the organizational level. The laptop is an ideal example of where these two worlds meet, and how to connect them. Mobile computing has become so powerful and flexible—used one moment to administer a million-dollar corporate website from the beach, the next to post vacation photos on your Facebook wall—that effectively protecting the information on the device requires the application of every mind-set explored in this book. And that's what makes the laptop an ideal training vehicle: you use it at home, at work, and on the road. It contains personal information as well as company data, and it is quite possibly the single most profitable target for thieves. My best advice is to use it as a training tool, as it appeals to both the individual and business sides of our personalities. If you can educate your staff to avoid data theft from a laptop, or at least minimize the collateral damage, you are well on your way to building a Culture of Privacy.

14 Travel with Care: Business Trips and Vacations

Traveling safely and preventing data theft go hand in hand. Because we carry so much identity with us when we travel and are much less organized when on the road, and because thieves target travelers, the likelihood of identity theft or data breach increases drastically while we're on vacation or traveling for business.

A Dream Vacation Turns into a Nightmare

You are planning the vacation of your dreams on the back end of a business trip to Europe. You can almost taste the pasta Bolognese you read about at that out-of-the-way trattoria halfway down an ancient blind alley in Tuscany.

But there's one area you overlooked that can turn that long-anticipated adventure into a nightmare: The potential theft of your most-valuable travel companion—your identity.

Fast-forward: You found the trattoria, and have savored the last bite of pasta, drained your pitcher of vino rosso, and happily presented your debit card to the waiter. He looks concerned as he walks back to your table to tell you that your card has been declined. It doesn't take long to discover that a thief has emptied your bank account and there is nothing left to pay for your dream vacation. Likewise, you discover, your credit cards are useless, frozen tight due to maxed-out credit limits. Hopefully, you have a backup plan (cash) to pay for the meal. Hopefully, the thief hasn't also

(continued)

(continued)

stolen your passport and isn't travelling under your identity with complete immunity.

But the news only worsens when you get back to your hotel room. You haven't thought much about your laptop computer since you completed your business obligations days ago and became preoccupied with exploring. Now you realize your laptop is missing, and with it, thousands of pieces of customer identity. Your vacation is over, and your carelessness has caused not only your pain but someone else's as well. You'll be lucky to save your job.

Travel is where the worlds of personal and corporate data loss commonly overlap, and so can be difficult to distinguish. Passports can be stolen in the same moment as customer files or laptop computers. The time you spend recovering identity on a business trip can translate into thousands of dollars for your company. The point is, traveling with care benefits individuals and businesses alike. Preparing wisely to protect identity can save you money, and prevent headaches, while on your trip.

Before You Leave Home

Follow these three guidelines before you walk out the door (the associated mind-sets are enclosed in parentheses):

1. Travel Light (Eliminate)

Simplify and minimize what you bring with you. Take only those identity items that are absolutely necessary. If possible, leave the following items behind when you travel:

- *Laptops.* As discussed in Chapter 13, "Protect Mobile Data," the safest place for your laptop while traveling is locked up at work or home. Unfortunately, this is not practical for most business travelers; it is, however, very practical on vacations. If you must have access to your e-mail, use your iPhone or BlackBerry.
- *Client Files.* Take with you only those parts of client files that are necessary. Don't automatically grab the entire file for any one project or client;

by doing so you are increasing exponentially the amount of data that can be stolen.

- *Company Data.* Leave financials, trade secrets, intellectual capital, customer lists, employee records, organization charts, and sales and marketing strategies in the office whenever possible. These may be in the form of paper documents, USB thumb drives, CDs, DVDs, SD cards, or other media. If this data is highly sensitive, you are safer storing it on a well-encrypted laptop.

- *Checks and Checkbooks.* Resist the temptation to carry checks; or take only one or two for an emergency, and carry them with your cash in your money belt. Checking account takeover is one of the simplest crimes to commit and one of the most devastating types of financial fraud from which to recover. The easy alternative? Use a credit card or cash.

- *Debit Cards.* You can reduce your vulnerability to having your checking account emptied while on vacation by leaving all debit cards (check cards) at home. Don't be lulled into thinking that debit/ATM cards are safe just because they require a PIN or password. In fact, the only time a PIN is needed to use the card is when it is being used at an ATM. PINs are often not required when used at a store as a debit or credit card. Be aware, too, that debit cards don't have the same financial fraud protections as most credit cards. The solution? Ask your bank for an ATM-only debit card (you can't use it in stores, only at cash machines) and make sure your password isn't overseen when you are at an ATM. Regardless, it is best to use a credit card or cash. The exception to this is when you are traveling in a foreign country and your debit card is the most economical method of obtaining cash from an ATM.

- *Extra Credit Cards.* Every piece of identity you take with you represents another source of potential fraud to which you are exposed. If you are traveling with another adult, I recommend that you each take one credit card (from two separate credit card companies). Notify your credit card company of the dates and places where you are traveling, so that it doesn't shut down your card when charges are made out of town. Also, make sure you have a large enough credit line to cover your purchases while traveling.

- *Social Security Cards and Other Identity Documents.* You do not need your Social Security card while traveling (or at any time other than your first day of work with a new employer), so leave it locked up at home. Leave birth certificates, passports (unless travelling internationally), library cards, receipts, and so on at home while you travel. The rule of thumb is: Leave anything you don't *absolutely* need locked away at home (*Lock*). If you can travel with only a credit card, driver's license, and health insurance card (as long as it doesn't have your SSN on it), you will be much safer.

- *Bills.* Don't take bills to pay with you while traveling. Instead, set up electronic bill pay through your bank, or pay these bills before you leave town.

2. Protect Your Home (Accumulate)

There are a few layers of protection to implement before leaving town to help ensure that your home, valuables, and other important belongings will be safe while you are away. Identity theft is one of the most common reasons burglaries are committed while people are away from home.

- *Hold newspapers and mail (Eliminate).* Your mailbox is an identity bonanza. Before you leave, place a "postal hold" on your mail so that your mailbox isn't vulnerable while you are gone. Arrange with your post office that only you (or your spouse) can pick up your mail. Don't have it "mass-delivered" the day after you return, as this puts everything at risk all at once. Instead, pick it up at the post office when you return to town.
- *Make it look like you are home when you're not (Defend).* Leave a light on here or there in the house, or put a main light on a timer, set to turn on at the same time every day. Ask a neighbor to remove any fliers that may accumulate at the front door, and bring in trash cans from the street. This will give the impression that you are home even when you are away for weeks at a time.
- *Lock all entry points (Lock).* Lock all windows and doors securely. Fix any broken or damaged locks before you leave, and cover up any doggie doors or other entry points into your home. Lock your identity documents and other valuables in a bolted-down fire safe or safe room.
- *Photocopy the contents of your wallet (Monitor).* This includes your passport if you are traveling internationally. Give one copy to a trusted friend or relative while you are away so that he or she can send you the necessary information in an emergency. Bring another copy with you, and carry it in a secure place while you travel. This simple step will save you hours of frustration if anything is lost or stolen.

- *Don't publicize your trip on social networking sites (Defend)*. Don't post an "Away on Vacation" note on your Facebook, MySpace, or Twitter pages, or on any other social networking site. Broadcasting this information is tantamount to inviting criminals to use that information while you are away. As a general rule, you should think twice about any information you share on social networking sites. Suspend your account on location-based social networking sites like FourSquare.com that alert thieves that you are traveling.

3. Protect Your Office (Accumulate)

Your home isn't the only target of theft while you are away traveling. You need to take similar steps before leaving your office.

- *Physically lock up your computer (Lock)*. Physically limiting access to your computer while you are away is the easiest and best way to protect your system and system-stored passwords.
- *Clean your desk (Eliminate)*. Remove all data, physical and digital, from your desk. Place it in a locking filing cabinet or other secure place.
- *Lock your office door (Lock)*. Don't overlook this simple, very effective step. If you think someone might need access into the office while you are gone, leave a copy of the key with someone you trust completely. Make that person the gatekeeper to your office while you are away.

During Travel

Three guidelines apply while you're on the road, too.

1. Lock It Up (Lock and Secure)

I can't stress enough the importance of using the in-room safes that are now features of most hotel rooms. Hanging a "Do Not Disturb" sign on the door-knob is no guarantee that the hotel staff will not enter the room. *Always* use the in-room safe to store anything of value. They are simple to use and drastically increase traveling safety. Also, make sure all of your electronic devices are password-protected. Lock up the following items:

- *Laptop Computers (Lock and Secure):* Carry your laptop with you only when absolutely necessary. The rest of the time, place your laptop (or just the hard drive if your laptop is too big) in the safe when you aren't using it. Before using your laptop to access online banking or other password-protected services from Wi-Fi networks, verify that the Wi-Fi hot spots are secure.

- *Client Files (Eliminate and Lock):* Unless it is absolutely necessary, don't travel with any client files. They might not seem particularly sensitive until they go missing and a client sues your company. Take only those individual documents that you will need and leave the rest locked up in your office.

- *Public-Access Internet Facilities (Secure):* If you plan to use a public computer in hotel business centers or cybercafés, never access any sensitive information on them. Keylogging software can track your keystrokes, which lets thieves follow everything you are doing.

- *Cell Phones (Lock):* When you go down to a conference meeting or off to the pool, store your cell phone in the safe, along with your laptop, passport, jewelry, extra cash, iPod, thumb drive, and other valuables.

- *Passports (Lock):* Unless you are traveling in a country where you are required to keep your passport with you at all times, lock it up in the safe the entire time you are staying at the hotel.

- *Other Identity Documents (Lock):* Store your plane tickets, receipts, and any other identity documents (birth certificates, extra credit cards, visa, etc.) in the safe when not in use.

2. Carry Your Belongings Safely

When you cannot keep your important documents, cash, credit cards, and passports in a secure safe, carry them with you in a secure way.

- *Carry a travel pouch (Lock):* Put all of your identity documents (passport, credit card, driver's license, tickets, etc.) in a travel pouch that fits around your neck or your waist (and inside your clothing), when they are not locked in a safe. This is a minor inconvenience, yes, but it lowers the risk of both pickpocketing and unintentional misplacement. Thieves have unbelievably nimble fingers, which they can slip into your pocket or purse undetected, so just before you leave your hotel room (especially in cities), verify that your money pouch is securely fastened around your waist or neck, under your clothes. Also, keep some change or a small amount of cash in a different and easily accessible inner pocket. You don't want to reveal where you keep your travel pouch when paying for a $5 train ticket in a public area.

● *Use a backpack (Lock):* When possible, carry laptops and other large identity-storing items in a backpack that stays zipped and on your back at all times. It is easy to set down a purse, book bag, or piece of luggage while at a ticket counter or retail store. Backpacks, on the other hand, are easy to keep on our person at all times, and are harder to break into without alerting the wearer. When traveling in a very crowded city, or on a subway, or at a train station or airport, consider wearing your backpack in front of you instead of on your back.

● *Don't lose sight of your credit cards (Monitor):* When paying with a credit card in a restaurant or store, try to keep your eye on the card. If the server removes it from sight, he or she may be able to create a "clone" by using a portable card skimmer that will copy the information from the card's magnetic strip. Many restaurants are now able to process the card at your table; or take it to the register, where you can observe the transaction.

3. Bank Safely (Monitor)

Use your ATM-only card (one that requires a PIN and does not contain a Visa or MasterCard logo) at cash machines located in banks or credit unions and that are in well-lit areas. Be sure to examine the ATM machine carefully for signs of tampering. Be on the lookout for anything that looks suspicious. Save all transaction receipts in an envelope for that purpose, to make it easy to reconcile your bank statement when you arrive home.

Upon Returning Home

As soon as possible after you return home, take these protective measures:

● *Monitor your accounts (Monitor):* While traveling, and as soon as possible after you return from your trip, pay special attention to your account statements, to make sure that nothing out of the ordinary appears. If a credit card number or bank account number was stolen during your trip, this is how you will catch it early and keep it from becoming a waking nightmare. Contact your provider and alert the representative to the breach immediately.

- *Rotate your account numbers (Eliminate):* If you suspect your identity might have been compromised (e.g., your credit card number stolen) while you were traveling, call your financial institution and ask to be issued a new card. This makes the old number obsolete, should anyone try to use it in the future.

- *Pick up your mail (Eliminate):* Don't leave your mail in anyone else's hands any longer than necessary. Don't forget to shred any mail that you don't need to keep.

- *Retrieve copies of identity documents (Monitor):* Retrieve any copies of your credit cards, driver's license, and passport that you gave to a trusted friend or relative, and shred them. There is no reason to keep those extra copies once you have returned home safely from your trip.

Like physical safety, data safety has become a necessary part of preparing to travel. By spending a few minutes protecting private information before, during, and after your travels, you will be sure to fully enjoy your time away.

Action Item Checklist: Travel with Care

- ☐ Travel light; simplify and minimize what you bring with you.
- ☐ Take precautions to protect your home.
- ☐ Take precautions to protect your office.
- ☐ Travel with a copy of your identity documents, and give a copy to a trusted friend.
- ☐ While traveling, securely lock up client files, laptops, cell phones, passports, and other identity documents.
- ☐ Carry a travel pouch, use a backpack, and keep an eye on your credit cards while out of your hands when traveling.
- ☐ Don't announce you are traveling on social networking sites.
- ☐ Bank safely, using well-lit ATMs in bank or credit union buildings.
- ☐ When you return home, monitor your bank accounts, and possibly rotate your account numbers.
- ☐ Pick up your mail as soon as possible; likewise, retrieve any copies of identity documents that you left with friends.

Business Relevance

All of the suggestions on the previous page apply equally to individuals traveling on vacation and businesspeople traveling for work. The difficulty for corporations is that people are naturally inclined to protect their own possessions (e.g., home, valuables, identity), but less willing to take the necessary extra steps when it comes to sensitive company information (which generally belongs to someone else). In other words, it is imperative that you find a way to make your executives and employees take *ownership* for company data.

In many ways, this requires the same skills that managers use to establish buy-in to sales targets, quarterly numbers, customer retention and so on. Building a Culture of Privacy requires a system of assigning responsibility, monitoring accountability, rewarding success and minimizing mistakes. Incorporating a reward/training program for compliance/non-compliance reinforces the mission critical nature of data safety in a positive manner.

For example, performing a periodic laptop spot check on an employee's computer prior to their travels accomplishes several things. First, it sends a definitive message that privacy matters to the organization. If the spot check turns out favorable, the responsible employee might be given a gift card for use during his or her trip. Second, it clearly delineates the consequences if the employee and laptop fail the inspection. Consequences should be determined on a business by business basis, but the most effective consequence I have witnessed is when the employee is required to do further training about the importance of privacy. This isn't meant to be a punishment, but a positive, educational response to inadequately fulfilling company requirements. The employee quickly learns how to protect the company asset (and keep themselves out of further training).

Recover Your Identity: When All Else Fails

This chapter lists the first and most crucial steps you must take if you are a victim of identity theft. It is important that you consult other resources and take more detailed action for your individual situation.

Consumers are spending considerably more time on fraud resolution, up to an average of 30 hours in 2008. This increase may be attributed to the increased sophistication of fraud schemes.

—*"2009 Identity Fraud Survey Report,"*
Javelin Strategy & Research

Most cases of identity theft are discovered by the victim, which reinforces the importance of monitoring your various accounts for suspicious behavior. Here is a list of the 15 most common warning signs suggesting that you might be a victim of identity theft or data breach.

Top 15 Ways to Detect Identity Theft

1. You receive a data breach notice in the mail from a company you do business with.
2. Your bills or statements are not arriving in your mail (or e-mail) on time.
3. You notice unauthorized charges on your credit card bill or debit card statement.
4. You notice new accounts or erroneous information on your credit report.

5. You are denied credit for a purchase.
6. You receive credit card bills for cards you don't own.
7. You are contacted by a collection agency about an item you didn't purchase.
8. You receive bills for unknown purchases, rental agreements, or services.
9. Businesses won't accept your check or credit card.
10. You are unable to set up new bank, loan, or brokerage accounts.
11. You notice withdrawals on your checking, savings, or brokerage account that you didn't make.
12. The checks listed on your bank statements don't reconcile with those listed in your check register. Many times these checks are made out to "Cash."
13. You notice a downward trend in benefits on your annual Social Security statement.
14. The police show up at your door.
15. A subpoena to appear in court arrives in the mail.

Action Items Checklist: Take Action Now

As you go through this checklist, I recommend that you keep a log of every step you have taken, whom you spoke with, the date and time of your conversation, and the results of your call. This log of contacts will become part of your dossier and will help you prove your financial, civil, and criminal innocence, should they be questioned. I also strongly suggest that you take these steps in order (there are 17), as several of them become more difficult once your credit is frozen. Finally, I urge you to take the first five within 24 hours of the theft or suspected theft.

1. Deactivate the Affected Accounts

If it is a specific account that you believe has been violated, shut that account down first. For example, if your credit card has been stolen, alert that credit card company and deactivate the card. Don't necessarily cancel the card yet, as doing so might make it more difficult to track the crime. If it is a bank or brokerage account, have the company suspend all capabilities on the account until you notify a representative of next steps. For credit cards, under federal law, you only responsible for a maximum of $50—if you report the fraudulent charges immediately.

Eventually, you will want to obtain a new credit card number, account number, password on the account, and so on; or potentially cancel the account altogether. When you are speaking to the financial institution, explain to the agent that a thief has used your identity and direct him/her to suspend or close the account. You can also request more details about the unauthorized account or use of the account, since the company will know more than you do. Request that any negative entries be removed from your credit report. You may be required to send an ID Theft Affidavit or other documentation. Make sure you follow up with the company; and as an added measure of protection, also submit this request in writing and keep a copy for your records.

For bank accounts, you will probably have to visit your local branch to cancel the old accounts and set up the new ones. Don't delay in doing this as the bank only covers theft that is reported in a "reasonable" amount of time.

100% of banks surveyed adopted zero-liability policies for signature debit purchases, and 96% of the top twenty-five financial institutions offer zero-liability for PIN debit purchases.

—"2009 Identity Fraud Survey Report,"
Javelin Strategy & Research

2. Alert New Creditors About Fraud

Immediately contact all new creditors that have been set up fraudulently. If the identity thief took out a home loan, call the loan agency and alert them to the problem. Request that they close the account or transfer it to a new account number immediately. They may ask for supporting documents, such as fraud affidavits and police reports (see numbers 4 and 5, respectively). If debt collectors contact you, respond immediately in writing and keep a copy of your letters. Explain that you are the victim of identity theft and that you don't owe the money. You have the right to ask the debt collectors for the name of the business that is owed the debt. Include your theft or fraud affidavit and a copy of the police report with your letter. Immediately contact the creditors and explain what happened; offer to send them your police report and ID Theft Affidavit.

3. Place a Fraud Alert on Your Credit File

Immediately place a fraud alert with all three credit-reporting bureaus (I list their phone numbers and websites at the end of this entry). A fraud alert requests that creditors contact you before issuing credit or opening new accounts in your name. If you report it to one bureau, it is supposed to report it to the other two. However, this could take days or weeks, so play it safe and report it to each agency yourself. Keep in mind, this is only a temporary solution. You will be freezing your credit in an upcoming step, but that is not always an immediate process; the fraud alert will lower your liability and increase your safety until the freeze takes effect. Make sure to cover the following points with the credit bureaus:

- Let them know that your identity is being used by a criminal to fraudulently obtain credit in your name.
- Ask them to place a fraud alert on your credit file. This is temporary and will last for 90 to 180 days only. I recommend that you eventually take the additional step of *freezing your credit.*
- Instruct them to add a victim's statement to your report; for example: "My identity has been stolen and used to fraudulently apply for credit. Please call me at [your phone number—cell phones are generally best because you carry them with you] to verify all applications."
- Verify with the bureau that you will be receiving a *current copy of your credit report* as well as instructions on how to file an extended multiyear fraud alert, should you want one. Review your credit file thoroughly to expose any fraudulent new accounts or existing account abuse.

Equifax: 1–800–525–6285; www.equifax.com.
Experian: 1–888–397–3742; www.experian.com.
TransUnion: 1–800–680–7289; www.transunion.com.

4. Submit an ID Theft Affidavit

The Federal Trade Commission (FTC) makes a copy of this document available at www.FTCComplaintAssistant.gov, or call 1–877–438–4338. Make sure you keep a copy for your files because you will use this document repeatedly in the next few weeks.

5. File a Police Report

Report the crime to your local police department immediately upon realizing it has been committed. The chances that they will pursue the criminal are small, but you need a copy of the police report to begin proving your innocence to creditors and law enforcement agencies. I warn you, some law enforcement agencies see so much identity theft these days that they make filling out a report quite a chore for the victim. Stick with it until you have a legitimate report in hand. Make sure that you bring the following items with you to include in your report:

- A copy of the FTC ID theft complaint
- A copy of a government-issued ID and proof of residency (e.g., a utility bill)
- Any fraudulent account numbers that were established, as far as you know them
- Any and all documented proof you have that the accounts are fraudulent
- Any information that you have on the thief or the crime

Don't leave the police station without getting a copy of the report; you will need it repeatedly during the process of straightening out your credit and addressing legal issues.

6. Sign Up for Identity Theft Monitoring

I highly recommend identity theft monitoring services if you have been a victim of identity theft, as it will afford you an extra level of identity surveillance. Should the thief use your identity again in the future, you will have a far better chance of catching it early if you are using monitoring services. (To learn more about monitoring services, please visit www.Sileo.com/productreviews.) It is important that you take this step *before* you freeze your credit; if you do it beforehand, it will make the sign-up process more difficult. If you already have a reputable identity theft monitoring service, contact it immediately to help you resolve your case of identity theft. Most of the services include recovery and restoration services as part of their offerings. Some of them will even help you restore your identity if you sign up for their service after the theft. But don't take any chances: sign up for identity monitoring before you become a victim.

7. Monitor Statements Very Closely

Since you know that at least one financial account has been violated, make sure that you monitor other accounts for similar abuse. Many victims find that their identities are being used for multiple fraudulent purposes and catch the additional crimes by closely monitoring their statements.

8. Contact Check Verification Services

Contact your bank to place stop payments on all missing checks. If your checks were stolen, or new checking accounts were established in your name, call the check verification companies and report the fraudulent checks. Here are their phone numbers:

- Certegy Check: 1–800–770–3792
- ChexSystems: 1–800–428–9623
- CrossCheck: 1–800–552–1900
- Global Payments: 1–866–850–9061
- National Check Fraud Service: 1–843–571–2143
- Shared Check Authorization Network: 1–800–262–7771
- TeleCheck: 1–800–366–2425

9. Freeze Your Credit (or Extend Your Fraud Alerts)

The best way to ensure that a thief cannot use your credit record anymore is to place a *security* or *credit freeze* on your account, as discussed in Chapter 4, "Eliminate the Source." A credit freeze places a password on your credit file, meaning that no one will have access to your information unless you grant it. Freezing your credit is free, though unfreezing it when you need to establish new credit sometimes requires a small fee (generally no more than $10).

Make sure that you wait until after you have resolved the identity theft issues to place a freeze on your credit, because doing so makes it more difficult for creditors to clean up the financial mess. Also be aware that a credit freeze can slow down your ability to apply for new credit in the future (by only a few minutes), but it is well worth the peace of mind it will give you.

If you do not wish to freeze your credit, I recommend that you extend your fraud alerts. After you receive your credit reports, follow the instructions from each bureau on how to extend your fraud alert for a longer period of time. You will generally have to submit your request for this in writing, and may need to include supporting documentation such as a fraud affidavit or police report. Make sure you reference the unique ID number that the bureau assigns to your case, and use certified, return-receipt mail when you send the requests. This is how you will know that the bureaus are processing your request and that action is being taken. Fraud alerts can be removed from your account at any time.

In your written letters to each bureau, request:

- The names and phone numbers of the credit grantors that were fraudulently established by the identity thief. This will save you time researching contact information.
- That the bureaus remove inquiries on your account that appeared as a result of the fraudulent activities.
- That the bureaus remove fraudulent accounts if you include a copy of the police report, if you live in one of the states where the bureaus are required to do this.
- That the bureaus notify any companies that have received your erroneous credit reports in the past few months, to alert them to the disputed information.

When you have been granted an extended alert, you are allowed two free copies of everything in your credit file for the first 12 months. Take advantage of the second report to confirm that you have cleared everything to your satisfaction.

Please be aware that these measures will not necessarily stop new fraudulent accounts from being established by the identity thief. Credit issuers (credit card companies, car dealers, lending companies, etc.) *are not required by law to observe fraud alerts*. Consequently, it is your responsibility to monitor your credit report from this point, on with increased diligence to spot any suspicious activity.

10. File an Identity Theft Victim's Report with the FTC

Visit www.Consumer.gov/idtheft to learn how to file an identity theft report and to verify that you have taken all of the steps suggested by the Federal Trade Commission.

11. Notify the Postal Inspector

If you know or suspect that you are the victim of mail theft or a fraudulent change of address, contact the Postal Inspector's Office, U.S. Post Office, at 1–800–275–8777 to obtain your regional number. You should also consider renting a locking mailbox or P.O. box, and drop off any sensitive outgoing mail to USPS collection boxes.

12. Contact the Social Security Administration

If your Social Security number has been stolen and is being used to exploit your benefits or commit unemployment fraud, contact the SSA. Report fraud to the agency's hotline at 1–800–269–0271, or visit the SSA website at www .SSA.gov. You can also visit your local Social Security office for a replacement card, if necessary. While you are there, ask about any additional steps you should take in response to a stolen Social Security card.

13. Contact the Passport Office

Whether or not you have a passport, alert the passport office to alert them to the potential of fraudulent passport applications being submitted in your name. Reach the passport office at www.Travel.State.gov/Passport/ Passport_1738.html.

14. Secure Your Phone Service

Call your phone companies (local, cell, and long distance) and ask them to password-protect your accounts. It is advisable to follow this same step with every company with which you conduct financial transactions.

15. Safeguard Your Driver's License

If someone is using your driver's license number to write bad checks, contact your state's Department of Motor Vehicles (DMV) to see if another license has been issued in your name. Instruct them to place a fraud alert on your license, if possible. If not, ask about the procedure in your state for filing a complaint. You can find your local office at www.OnlineDMV.com.

16. Visit the Theft Resource Center

If you have been the victim of identity theft, I urge you to pay a visit to the Identity Theft Resource Center website, at www.IDTheftCenter.org. This consumer-oriented website provides many victim resources, including guides, contacts, laws, and detailed information to help you in the recovery process.

17. Consider Hiring an Attorney

If you continue to have problems proving your identity, or cannot resolve the damage done by the identity thief, consider hiring an attorney to help clear your name.

One of the greatest motivators for protecting your identity is to see how much more work it is to recover from this crime than to avoid it in the first place. If your identity has been stolen and your recovery process is complete, don't do what I did and convince yourself that it won't happen again. Use what you have been through as fuel to keep it from happening again. I promise, you won't be sorry.

Business Relevance

The business equivalent of recovering from identity theft is recovering from data breach. But data breach brings with it a great deal more cost and responsibility for a variety of reasons:

- State and federal compliance laws dictate that the organization (e.g., corporation, association, university, or governmental department) notify every affected customer of the breach and take meaningful steps to rectify the situation. That can be interpreted in many different ways, but all of them add up to the same basic conclusion: the average breach recovery cost runs about $204[1] per breached record.
- Companies that experience breach generally end up on television, or on the front page of the paper. Poor publicity erodes the public's

trust in the offending company and often leads to customer defection, stock value decline and legal lawsuits.

- In addition to covering the costs of recovery, the offending company is simultaneously forced to implement the privacy principles outlined in this book and elsewhere in order to protect against future breach. Instead of accumulating security over time (and spreading the investment), public perception demands that they resolve their weaknesses immediately. Just like any complex task that must be completed quickly, rushing to build a Culture of Privacy on an already declining company will almost certainly compromise the strength of the solution, and will definitely cost more.

Recovering from, or even preparing for, a data breach is more detailed than the scope of this book. I recommend that you hire professional breach planning and response consultants to develop a breach response plan (or to respond to a breach that has already taken place). There are too many legal, financial, and ethical sinkholes along the way to be able to navigate it without an experienced partner. In the short term, it will cost your company more. But in the long term, you will recover more completely and correctly and will live to do business another day.

16

Prioritize Your Attack: The Privacy Calendar

This chapter lists all of the action items that are important to take to protect your identity. In the Privacy Calendar, however, they are listed by priority rather than mind-set. The order was determined according to three criteria:

1. Which steps need to be taken first to make the process simple?
2. Which actions are most effective at preventing identity theft?
3. Which items are you most likely to complete given time and resource constraints?

The detailed information for taking each of the steps given in this chapter is contained in the individual mind-set chapters, which are shown in italics and enclosed in parentheses following the steps, for easy identification. Salient points of each step are shown in boldface. I strongly recommend that you refer back to each chapter for in-depth explanations of each step.

I also highly recommend that you set up a schedule for yourself and complete the items phase by phase. Take 10 minutes a day, one hour per week, or one weekend a month and schedule time to "accumulate privacy." If you have to wait on one of the action items—for example, you order your credit report but it will be 10 days before you receive it—move on to another of the items further down the list and return to the item you skipped when you receive the report.

I've said it before, but it bears repeating: There is no silver bullet in the world of fraud or identity theft prevention. If someone tells you there is, he or she is probably trying to sell you something. Rather, the layered approach enumerated here will provide you with a base level of privacy, which you can add to over time.

For an electronic version of the Privacy Calendar (with live links), visit www.Sileo.com/privacy-calendar. Go there now to implement Phase 1.

Phase 1: Credit

1. Order and monitor your **free credit report**, and set up regular calendar reminders every four months to review your updated report. This can be completed online at www.AnnualCreditReport.com or by calling 1–877–322–8228. This step is not necessary if you take step 2 and subscribe to an identity monitoring service, which has the added benefit of providing convenient, consistent surveillance delivered directly to your e-mail box. (*Monitor*)

2. Sign up for a reputable **identity monitoring service** with 3-in-1 credit monitoring, cybertracking, theft restoration services, and recovery insurance. To learn more about specific surveillance products, visit www. Sileo.com/productreviews. (*Monitor*)

3. **Freeze your credit** with Equifax, Experian, and TransUnion. This step, while the most important for protecting your credit, makes it more difficult to take the two previous steps, which is why it is listed third. Visit www.FinancialPrivacyNow.com to begin the process. If you do not wish to place a security freeze on your credit, at least place an extended fraud alert on your file. (*Eliminate*)

4. Set up **online account alerts** for all of your banking, credit card, mortgage, and investment accounts. At the same time, reduce at-risk mail and switch to **online statements**, which allow you to easily and consistently monitor your accounts for signs of fraud. Begin using **online bill-pay** instead of sending checks through the mail. (*Monitor*)

Phase 2: Wallet

1. **Protect your wallet** or purse by keeping it with you or locked up at all times and by removing the following items (*Eliminate*):
   - Social Security card
   - Checks

- PIN numbers and passwords
- Excess credit and debit cards
- Credit card receipts
- ATM receipts and bank deposit slips
- Any cards containing a Social Security number that you are not required to carry

2. Sign your credit cards and include **Photo ID Required** on both the back and front. (*Eliminate*)
3. **Photocopy** every piece of identity in your wallet and store the copies safely, in case the wallet is stolen and you need to shut down accounts quickly. (*Eliminate*)

Phase 3: Databases

1. **Opt out** of information sharing, telemarketing, and junk mail by visiting www.OptOutPreScreen.com or calling 1–888–5–OPT–OUT. (*Eliminate*)
2. Place your name on the National **Do Not Call** Registry by visiting www .DoNotCall.gov. (*Eliminate*)
3. Place your name on the Direct Marketing Association's **Do Not Mail** list by visiting www.DMAChoice.org. (*Eliminate*)

Phase 4: Computers

1. Physically **lock your computer** in a secure place when in transit or when you are not using it. (*Secure*)
2. Protect your desktop, laptop, or server computer with the following **software security tools** (preferably by hiring a professional to help you implement them) (*Secure*):
   - Sophisticated alphanumeric/symbol login password that you change regularly
   - Security software suite with antivirus and antispyware
   - Hardware or software firewall with a strong, unique password that you change regularly
   - Data backup software that consistently and automatically backs up your files
   - Up-to-date Internet browser, with pop-up blocker and phishing alerts enabled

- Automatic software updates and security patches for all programs, including operating system, antivirus, antispyware, pop-up blockers, and firewalls
- WPA2-encrypted wireless connection
- Encrypted hard drive
- Password protection software to protect online login information

3. Have your computer or cell phone **digitally shredded** or low-level formatted before selling, donating, or passing it on to someone else. (*Destroy*)
4. Visit www.Sileo.com/productreviews to learn more about the best tools to implement.

Phase 5: Mobile Computing

1. Define what is at risk on your mobile data devices. (*Protect*)
2. Verify acceptable use of your mobile data devices with your company. (*Protect*)
3. Control exposure and eliminate **unnecessary transport** of your mobile data devices. (*Protect*)
4. **Encrypt** individual data files, as well as your hard drive, SIM card, and SD memory card. (*Protect*)
5. Utilize a **secure wireless Internet** connection. (*Protect*)
6. Utilize **SSL-encrypted e-mail**, and e-mail sensitive data only when absolutely necessary. (*Protect*)
7. Use a backpack or other carrying case to keep your mobile devices physically on you. (*Protect*)
8. Consider adding a locking or **alarm device** to your laptop and mobile computing devices. (*Protect*)
9. When going through security at the airport, don't put your laptop on the X-ray belt until you are ready to walk through the metal detector; keep an eye on it until you reach the other side. (*Protect*)
10. Utilize a LoJack-type software program to **track your laptop** if it is stolen. (*Protect*)
11. **Password-protect** your cell phone and PDA with a sophisticated alphanumeric/symbol login. (*Eliminate*)
12. Destroy any sensitive files that you store electronically after you are done using them. (*Protect*)

Phase 6: Physical Documents

1. Purchase a high-quality, **cross-cut document shredder** and shred every document, disk, and credit card that you no longer need. Place the shredders conveniently, for easy access. (*Destroy*)
2. Create a **safe room**, or purchase a fire safe or fire-rated filing cabinet and have it secured to the foundation of your home or office. Lock your essential documents according to the chart. (*Lock*)
3. **Lock your mail** and mailbox against theft. (*Lock*)
   - Use a locking mailbox or get a P.O. box.
   - Mail sensitive documents in person.
   - Have identity documents sent by UPS or FedEx (with tracking).
   - Have new checks sent to your bank for pickup.
   - Retrieve mail within an hour or two after delivery and watch for new credit cards.

Phase 7: Online

1. **Research your online identity.** Google your name, phone number, address, e-mail address, and any other information you would like to verify. (*Defend*)
2. Withhold or **mask identity information** when building your social networking profile, including: date of birth, address, phone number(s), and any password reminders that you use (high school, city born, pet's name, etc.). (*Defend*)
3. Read and **understand your privacy settings** on Facebook, Twitter, LinkedIn, MySpace, and other social networking sites; adjust them to protect your identity information. (*Defend*)
4. **Vary online passwords** and make them more sophisticated by using alphanumeric/symbol passwords. (*Secure*)
5. Be alert and wary of **"friends in distress"** scams, posted links, and other social engineering scams. (*Defend*)
6. Only **"friend" your actual friends**, and understand both the benefits and drawbacks of responding to quizzes and surveys, and utilizing widgets, groups, and third-party applications, before you add them. (*Defend*)
7. Don't forget: **posts are permanent, public, and exploitable.** (*Defend*)
8. **Protect your e-mail** (*Defend*):

- Set your e-mail privacy and spam controls high.
- Never reply to a spam e-mail, even to request being removed.
- Research links before you click, including clickable images.
- Don't trust offers that seem too good to be true.
- Never enter personal or financial information into pop-up windows.

9. Become knowledgeable about **information collection** performed by search engines, cookies, and toolbars. (*Defend*)
10. Read, understand, and adjust your **application privacy settings** in Google, Google Docs, Gmail, Hotmail, Yahoo!, or other online accounts. (*Defend*)
11. Be aware and recognize **phishing scams**. (*Secure*)
12. **Shop securely** online, patronizing only reputable, recognizable companies. (*Secure*)

Phase 8: Travel

1. **Travel light**; simplify and minimize what you take with you. (*Travel*)
2. Take precautions to **protect your home and office** while away. (*Travel*)
3. Travel with a **copy of your identity** documents and give a second copy to a trusted friend. (*Travel*)
4. While traveling, securely **lock up** client files, laptops, cell phones, and passports and other identity documents. (*Travel*)
5. Carry a travel pouch, use a backpack, and watch your credit cards while out of your hands when traveling. (*Travel*)
6. Don't announce to strangers on social networking sites when you will be traveling. (*Travel*)
7. Bank safely, using only **well-lit ATMs** in banks or credit union buildings. (*Travel*)
8. When you return home, **monitor your bank accounts** and possibly rotate your account numbers. If possible and safe to do so, monitor your accounts while traveling. (*Travel*)
9. **Pick up your mail** as soon as possible after you return; likewise retrieve any copies of identity documents that you left with friends. (*Travel*)

Phase 9: Social Engineering

1. Learn to **observe** what is going on around you by slowing down. (*Evaluate*)

2. React to requests for identity of any type with **healthy skepticism.** (*Evaluate*)
3. Think "**Hogwash!**" when anyone tries to access your data. (*Evaluate*)
4. Look for signs of **manipulation** (fear, rushing, bribery, flattery, trust, security). (*Evaluate*)
5. **Stop, look, and listen** when your hogwash reflex triggers. (*Evaluate*)
6. When in doubt, **interrogate the enemy.** (*Evaluate*)
7. Implement the **four phases of interrogation** by asking four revealing questions (*Interrogate*):
   - Who is in **control** of this interaction?
   - Can the person requesting the information **justify** his or her legitimacy?
   - What **options** do I have other than sharing the data?
   - What are the **benefits** of the particular choice I am making?
8. Don't be afraid to say **no.** (*Interrogate*)

Phase 10: Extras

1. Create a **dossier**, complete with photocopies and logs of all crucial identity documents, for future reference. (*Monitor*)
2. Use an **electronic calendar** (like Microsoft Outlook) to track your billing cycles. (*Monitor*)
3. Guard against shoulder surfing (someone peering over your shoulder or recording you on a cell phone video camera) to steal your PIN while at an ATM or retail checkout. (*Evaluate*)
4. Monitor your annual **Social Security statement.** (*Monitor*)
5. Eliminate or lock up all identity documents in your **car.** (*Eliminate*)
6. Remove your name from other physical and **online directories.** (*Eliminate*)
7. **Scratch out** all but the last four digits of any unmasked credit card numbers on the merchant's copy of your credit card receipt. (*Destroy*)
8. Implement all safeguards for your **spouse or partner.** (*Secure*)

Resources

Information on John Sileo and The Sileo Group:
www.Sileo.com
www.PrivacyMeansProfit.com
www.ThinkLikeASpy.com

Information on Privacy Protection Products
www.Sileo.com/productreviews

Electronic Privacy Calendar
www.Sileo.com/privacy-calendar

Electronic Privacy Information
www.EFF.org
www.EPIC.org

Consumers Union: Financial Privacy Now
www.FinancialPrivacyNow.org

Federal Trade Commission: Identity Theft Site
www.FTC.gov/idtheft

ID Theft Resource Center
www.IDTheftCenter.org

Privacy Rights Clearinghouse
www.PrivacyRights.org

Notes

Part I   Boot Camp: Privacy Means Profit

Chapter 1   Motivate the Troops

1. "Estimates Put T.J. Maxx Security Fiasco At $4.5 Billion," *Information Week*, May 2, 2007, citing research conducted by IP Locks, a compliance and database security company, and the Ponemon Institute, an independent research company. www.informationweek.com/news/security/showArticle.jhtml?articleID= 199203 277.
2. www.finance.yahoo.com, February 24, 2009.
3. "Fifth Annual U.S. Cost of Data Breach Study," Ponemon Institute, 2010, p. 4.
4. "Data Breach Defense 2009," Javelin Strategy & Research, March 3, 2009.
5. "2009 Data Breach Investigations Report," Verizon Business, April 15, 2009.
6. "Data Breach Defense 2009," Javelin Strategy & Research, March 3, 2009.

Chapter 2   Define the Problem

1. "2009 Identity Fraud Survey Report," Javelin Strategy & Research, p. 42.
2. Ibid., p. 46.
3. "Fifth Annual U.S. Cost of Data Breach Study," Ponemon Institute, 2010, p. 4.

Part II   Basic Training: Think Like a Spy

Chapter 4   The First Mind-Set: Eliminate the Source

1. "2009 Identity Fraud Survey Report," Javelin Strategy & Research, p. 46.

Chapter 5   The Second Mind-Set: Destroy the Data

1. See *California v. Greenwood*, U.S. Citation 486 U.S. 35 (1988) Docket 86684: Conclusion: Voting 6 to 2, the Court held that garbage placed at the curbside is unprotected by the Fourth Amendment. The Court argued that there was no reasonable expectation of privacy for trash on public streets "readily accessible to

animals, children, scavengers, snoops, and other members of the public." The Court also noted that the police cannot be expected to ignore criminal activity that can be observed by "any member of the public."
2. "Security of Paper Documents in the Workplace," Ponemon Institute, October 2008, p. 5.

Chapter 6   The Third Mind-Set: Secure the Systems

1. "WPA2 Security Now Mandatory for Wi-Fi CERTIFIED Products," www.wi-fi.org/news_articles.php?f=media_news&news_id=16, March 13, 2006.
2. "2009 Identity Fraud Survey Report," Javelin Strategy & Research, p. 60.
3. "Fifth Annual U.S. Cost of Data Breach Study," Ponemon Institute, 2010, p. 5.

Chapter 7   The Fourth Mind-Set: Lock the Docs

1. Federal Trade Commission press release, www.ftc.gov/opa/2005/06/disposal.shtm, June 1, 2005.
2. "Security of Paper Documents in the Workplace," Ponemon Institute, October 2008, pp. 2, 5.

Chapter 9   The Sixth Mind-Set: Interrogate the Enemy

1. www.ponemon.org/blog/post/use-what-works-to-create-a-culture-of-privacy, December, 20, 2009.

Chapter 10   The Seventh Mind-Set: Monitor the Signs

1. "2009 Identity Fraud Survey Report," Javelin Strategy & Research, p. 58.

Part III   Field Combat: Target the Enemy

Chapter 11   Deploy Targeting Strategies: Accumulate, Prioritize, and Adapt

1. http://news.cnet.com/8301-13579_3-9914753-37.html
2. "Fourth Annual U.S. Cost of Data Breach Study," Ponemon Institute, January 2009, p. 7.
3. "Global State of Information Security Study, Javelin Strategy & Research, 2008.
4. "2009 Breach Report," Identity Theft Resource Center, 2009.
5. "Ponemon Business Case for Data Protection Report," Ponemon Institute, July 15, 2009, p. 3.

6. Ibid. Average cost savings or revenue improvements resulting from data protection efforts = $16 million. Average data protection spending = $3.7 million. ($16M – $3.7M) ÷ $3.7M = 332% ROI.

Chapter 12 Defend Online Identity: Social Networking and the Cloud

1. www.facebook.com/press/info.php?statistics, January 4, 2010.
2. Alessandro Acquisti and Ralph Gross, "Predicting Social Security Numbers from Public Data," *Proceedings of National Academy of Sciences of the United States* (PNAS) 106:10975–10980, 2009; published online before print version, July 6, 2009, doi: 10.1073/pnas.0904891106.
3. www.informationweek.com/news/security/privacy/showArticle.jhtml?articleID= 218400854, January 4, 2010.
4. Joseph Bonneau and Sören Preibusch, "The Privacy Jungle: On the Market for Data Protection in Social Networks," University of Cambridge, May 26, 2009, pp. 14–15.
5. http://bits.blogs.nytimes.com/2009/03/31/spam-back-to-94-of-all-e-mail, January 4, 2010.
6. www.google.com/corporate/history.html, January 4, 2010.
7. http://en.wikipedia.org/wiki/Google_Earth, January 4, 2010.
8. http://mail.google.com/mail/help/about_privacy.html, January 4,2010.
9. Robert Gellman, "Privacy in the Clouds," World Privacy Forum, February 23, 2009, p. 4.
10. Ibid., p. 6.
11. Ibid., p. 22.
12. Ibid., p. 11.
13. Ibid., p. 14.
14. Ibid., p. 7.
15. Ibid., p. 6.
16. Ibid., p. 9.

Chapter 13 Protect Mobile Data: Laptop Responsibility

1. See the Privacy Rights Clearinghouse website, www.PrivacyRightsClearingHouse .org, for further details.
2. "Fifth Annual U.S. Cost of Data Breach Study," Ponemon Institute, January, 2010, p. 22.

Chapter 15 Recover Your Identity: When All Else Fails

1. "Fifth Annual U.S. Cost of Data Breach Study", Ponemon Institute, 2010, p. 19.

Index

About the Author

John Sileo's identity was stolen from his small business and used to commit a series of crimes, including $300,000 worth of digital embezzlement. While the data thief operated behind the safety of John's identity, John and his business were held legally and financially responsible for the felonies committed. Ultimately, the data breach destroyed John's business and consumed two years of his life as he fought to stay out of jail. Then he chose to fight back and speak out.

Emerging from this crisis, John became America's leading professional speaker on information survival, including identity theft prevention, data security, and safe social networking. His experiences as victim *and* victor led him to write the critically acclaimed, award-winning book, *Stolen Lives: Identity Theft Prevention Made Simple* (Da Vinci Publications, 2005), which was selected as the number-one Business Book at the EVVY Awards. Since the day he was wrongly accused, John has been on a mission to educate businesses and individuals to take back control of their data privacy before it's too late.

John's satisfied clients include the Department of Defense, the Federal Trade Commission, the FDIC, Blue Cross/Blue Shield, Pfizer, the Federal Reserve Bank, Lincoln Financial Group, AARP, Prudential, Liberty Mutual, and scores of financial institutions, universities, and associations around the world. As a lifetime entrepreneur, John loves speaking to small businesses about achieving entrepreneurial prosperity. He frequently appears on NBC, ABC, and FOX, and writes for Dr. Laura.com and other publications.

John is president of The Sileo Group, an idea-lab focused on inspiring privacy and prosperity through keynote speaking, business coaching, and advanced seminars. He graduated with honors from Harvard University, and has served as a Rotary Ambassadorial Scholar to New Zealand. John lives